Dyslexia: A Complete Guide for Parents

Gavin Reid
University of Edinburgh, Scotland, UK

John Wiley & Sons, Ltd

Other Wiley Editorial Offices

John Wiley & Sons Inc., 111 River Street, Hoboken, NJ 07030, USA

Jossey-Bass, 989 Market Street, San Francisco, CA 94103-1741, USA

Wiley-VCH Verlag GmbH, Boschstr. 12, D-69469 Weinheim, Germany

John Wiley & Sons Australia Ltd, 33 Park Road, Milton, Queensland 4064, Australia

John Wiley & Sons (Asia) Pte Ltd, 2 Clementi Loop #02-01, Jin Xing Distripark, Singapore 129809

John Wiley & Sons Canada Ltd, 22 Worcester Road, Etobicoke, Ontario, Canada M9W 1L1

Wiley also publishes its books in a variety of electronic formats. Some content that appears in print may
not be available in electronic books.

Library of Congress Cataloging-in-Publication Data

Reid, Gavin, 1950–
    Dyslexia : a complete guide for parents / Gavin Reid.
        p. cm.
    Includes bibliographical references.
    1. Dyslexic children – Popular works.   2. Dyslexia – Popular works.   I. Title.
RJ496.A5R45   2005
618.92′8553 – dc22

                                                                        2004012531

British Library Cataloguing in Publication Data

A catalogue record for this book is available from the British Library

ISBN 0-470-86312-9

Typeset in 11/14pt Times New Roman by TechBooks, Pvt Ltd. New Delhi, India
Printed and bound in Great Britain by Antony Rowe Ltd, Chippenham, Wiltshire
This book is printed on acid-free paper responsibly manufactured from sustainable forestry
in which at least two trees are planted for each one used for paper production.

Dyslexia: A Complete Guide for Parents

Contents

About the author

Dr Gavin Reid is a Senior Lecturer in Educational Studies at the Moray House School of Education, University of Edinburgh. He is also the parent of a now young man with special needs, who was diagnosed at a young age. He is an experienced teacher, educational psychologist, university lecturer, author and researcher. He has made over 500 conference, seminar and workshop presentations throughout the UK, Norway, Denmark, Germany, Italy, USA, New Zealand, Australia, Hong Kong, Poland, Republic of Ireland, Slovakia, Croatia, Czech Republic, Estonia, Austria, Cyprus, Greece and Hungary. He has written and edited key course books for teacher training in the field of dyslexia and literacy. *Dyslexia: A Practitioner's Handbook,* 3rd edition (Wiley, 2003) is used as a course text in many university and college courses on dyslexia worldwide and has been widely welcomed by teachers. He has also written and edited other books, book chapters and articles on dyslexia and learning styles as well as co-developing screening tests to identify literacy and other specific difficulties.

Gavin Reid is a graduate of Aberdeen and Glasgow universities. He has taught in Secondary Schools in Aberdeen and was an Educational Psychologist in Aberdeenshire and Fife, Scotland, before joining the staff at Moray House in Edinburgh in 1991.

His current interests include working with parents and adults, assessment and learning. He is a director and consultant to the Red Rose School for children with specific learning difficulties in St Anne's on Sea, Lancashire, England. He is also a consultant to a number of national and international projects in dyslexia and has been involved in evaluation of provision for students with dyslexia in Scotland, England and Wales. He has been, and currently holds appointments as, external examiner to universities in Scotland, England and Australia. He is a member of the British Dyslexia Association Teacher Training Accreditation Board and has been involved as a consultant to other parent groups and charitable bodies in the UK, Europe and New Zealand. His website is www.gavinreid.co.uk.

Other books by Gavin Reid

Peer, L. & Reid, G. (Eds) (2000) *Multilingualism, Literacy and Dyslexia: A Challenge for Educators*. London: David Fulton Publishers.

Peer, L. & Reid, G. (Eds) (2001) *Dyslexia: Successful Inclusion in the Secondary School*. London: David Fulton Publishers.

Reid, G. (Ed.) (1996) *Dimensions of Dyslexia (Vol. 1): Assessment, Teaching and the Curriculum*. Edinburgh: Moray House Publications.

Reid, G. (Ed.) (1996) *Dimensions of Dyslexia (Vol. 2): Literacy, Language and Learning*. Edinburgh: Moray House Publications.

Reid, G. (2003) *Dyslexia: A Practitioner's Handbook* (3rd edn). Chichester: John Wiley & Sons.

Reid, G. (2004) *Dyslexia and Inclusion*. National Association Special Education Needs (NASEN).

Reid, G. & Fawcett, A. (Eds) (2004) *Dyslexia in Context: Research, Policy and Practice*. London: Whurr.

Reid, G. & Given, B. (1998) *Learning Styles: A Guide for Teachers and Parents*. St Anne's on Sea, Lancashire: Red Rose Publications.

Reid, G. & Kirk, J. (2001) *Dyslexia in Adults: Education and Employment*. Chichester: John Wiley & Sons.

Reid, G. & Wearmouth, J. (Eds) (2002) *Dyslexia and Literacy: Theory and Practice*. Chichester: John Wiley & Sons.

Weedon, C. & Reid, G. (2001) *Listening and Literacy Index – A Group Test to Identify Specific Learning Difficulties*. London: Hodder & Stoughton.

Weedon, C. & Reid, G. (2003) *Special Needs Assessment Profile (SNAP)*. London: Hodder Murray.

Preface

Parents have a key role in supporting children with dyslexia. This role can be more influential than that played by the school. Although the school has a major responsibility for meeting the needs of children with dyslexia, the emotional strength needed to cope with dyslexia and the motivation to succeed can often come from home. Children with dyslexia are individuals. They are different from each other and may also learn in a different way from other children. These differences need to be recognised and catered for within the education system. Parents have a role to play to help to foster and maintain constructive communication with the school. As a parent you have to put your trust in others. We are fortunate; the teachers who cater for our children's needs are usually highly trained, highly skilled and caring individuals and schools are increasingly welcoming parents as partners.

Yet for some parents these words above may sound slightly optimistic. Some parents have not had good experiences. Some have been frustrated at the lack of recognition of dyslexia; others have had to resort to expensive interventions; and some have witnessed first hand how their child has suffered unnecessarily on account of dyslexia.

There has, nevertheless, been considerable progress in recent years in both the recognition of dyslexia and in teaching approaches from which a considerable number of children and young people with dyslexia, and their families, have benefited. Sadly, some have not.

How schools cater for dyslexia differs from country to country and even within countries, and I have tried to highlight this by referring to situations in a number of areas. However, the main thrust of this book is to provide guidance to parents, wherever they live and whatever obstacles they, and their children, are facing. The challenges facing parents can be enormous, but while researching this book I have found that the supports available are also considerable. Organisations representing the needs of people with dyslexia and their families are influential. When I first became involved in dyslexia around 20 years ago, the main thrust of organisations was to lobby government to ensure that dyslexia was recognised in schools. Now governments recognise the expertise of such organisations and are readily consulting with them and seeking advice on what is appropriate and effective for children with dyslexia.

Legislation and technology are both on the side of dyslexia. Increasingly, countries are ensuring that the rights of all those with a disability of some type are recognised. For legislative purposes dyslexia is recognised as a disability, yet for many children and young people with dyslexia, it is a gift. They are able to construct and create and solve all sorts of difficulties in their own way, and can be an inspiration to others. Many have succeeded in a variety of careers and are living a fulfilling life. Some have become politicians, actors, journalists, teachers, doctors, authors, artists, technicians or engineers, to name just a few of the professions in which people with dyslexia have been known to succeed. The other side of the coin is also evident as research has shown that too many people with dyslexia have difficulty adjusting to the obstacles they face, and this can lead to antisocial behaviour. For that reason it is important that parents and schools work together, that parent groups continue to campaign for what they know to be right and for individual parents to recognise the supports, the emotional needs and the life skills required by young people with dyslexia.

The essence of this book is just that: to recognise the role parents play and to inform, support and advise them on how they can play that role. Often, after a child with dyslexia has been assessed, parents will immediately ask 'What can we do at home?' This is perfectly natural and there is a great deal that parents can do. It is important, however, that home and school are linked, and one of the key factors is, in fact, 'collaboration'. Technology, however, is on the side of dyslexia. Many families have home computers and an abundance of educational software is available, some developed primarily for dyslexia. Parents can also give a great deal by understanding their children with dyslexia, by recognising their style of learning and encouraging their talents and dreams, and by providing the stable emotional base that will stand them in good stead throughout life.

All those points have been noted throughout this book, which intends to give parents information and advice as well as encouragement and hope. There are chapters on understanding dyslexia and specifically on understanding how children with dyslexia learn. There are chapters on recognising dyslexia and on strategies and programmes that parents can use at home. There is information on legislation and support, and guidance on supporting a young person throughout the transition from schools to college and to work. The book also contains first-hand accounts of parents' views. Research conducted specifically for this book provides insights into parents' hopes, successes, dilemmas and, in some cases, despair. I would like to formally acknowledge the help and support I received from these parents, and from other friends and colleagues, while writing this book.

This book is mainly for parents. It will, however, also benefit those directly involved in education and help them to understand the needs of parents of children with dyslexia. Of course, ultimately the book is written on behalf of dyslexic children who, through the support of parents and the wider education and social community, will thrive, develop and maintain motivation for learning and fulfil their potential.

Chapter 1

An introduction to dyslexia

As a parent you may be the first to suspect that your son or daughter has dyslexia. You may feel there should have been more progress, the inquisitive spark you noticed in oral discussion seems to contrast with the reluctance and drudgery your child experiences with written work. He or she may have difficulty in acquiring basic skills in reading and spelling. School reports are not too good. You are worried. Will these difficulties result in loss of interest in learning? Are career and college aspirations out of the question? Will unhappiness set in as the failure to read translates into failure to perform in any subject in school and loss of motivation? Will hurdles, such as preparing for examinations and even completing homework, become insurmountable burdens?

For many parents, children and young people with dyslexia, these fears can be the reality. But it need not be! Children and adults with dyslexia can have much to offer and much to achieve both educationally and socially. This book, while identifying the hurdles that parents need to overcome, will also provide a positive message – one of hope and opportunity, of support and success and of acceptance and achievement. The awareness of dyslexia among teachers, head teachers, classroom assistants, employers and university and college staff has increased considerably in most countries. Now there is good reason for hope as increasing opportunities for success are now available for all young people with dyslexia.

I have interviewed many parents to gather information for this book and heard some harrowing accounts of despair and disappointment. Some parents have had to take on the role of professionals just to ensure that their child is properly diagnosed. There are parents in California who paid for their son's teacher to attend a dyslexia conference because the school did not see it as a priority. There are parents in New Zealand who travelled halfway across the world for an assessment of their child's needs. There is a parent in the UK who had to go as far as the European courts to ensure that her child received an adequate educational placement. Such accounts can probably fill this book, but that is not necessary, nor is it the purpose of this book. Certainly in each of these accounts of despair there will be some common factors and shared concerns, and these shared concerns will be the focus of this book. This book will therefore be appropriate for parents in every country and the information chapter at the end of the book (Chapter 9) will also provide specific guidance for parents in different countries.

Dyslexia: some points to consider

As a parent – especially if you have only recently discovered that your child is dyslexic – the way forward, and perhaps even the explanation you are offered of dyslexia, can be conflicting and confusing. You may be surprised and anxious at the reluctance of some professionals to use the term 'dyslexia'. You may be puzzled by the ambiguities and disagreements among researchers. Yet there are some key points that should be explained to parents in relation to exactly what dyslexia is and the implications for their child's education and social and personal development.

This book will cover these implications. To begin with, however, some key points in relation to the characteristics of dyslexia are indicated below.

Dyslexia is individual – This means that children with dyslexia may have slightly different characteristics from each other. These characteristics can have a varying impact on the child. In some children this may not be too noticeable, but in others it can be very obvious. Dyslexia, therefore, can be evident within a continuum from mild to severe.

This, of course, means that what works for one dyslexic child may not work successfully for another.

Dyslexia relates to how information is processed – This means that dyslexia involves more than reading, but affects learning and how all information – including oral instructions – is learned. This will be explained in more detail in Chapter 3 of this book. It is essential to recognise at this point, however, that the cycle of learning, called the 'information processing cycle', is important. This can help us to understand the difficulties experienced by children with dyslexia. This cycle applies to how we take information in, how we memorise it and how we display to others that we know it.

Children with dyslexia can have difficulty in displaying knowledge and understanding in written work – In school performances, children usually display what they know through the written mode. Yet this may be the dyslexic child's weakest way of presenting information. Writing can be laborious and tedious for the dyslexic child, but it can be made easier and more enjoyable if he or she is provided with a structure for writing, and perhaps even the key words. One of the important points to consider here is that we need to identify and acknowledge the specific strengths of the child with dyslexia.

Children with dyslexia can have difficulty learning through the auditory modality, i.e. through listening – There are many ways of learning, particularly today with computer games and other electronic learning and leisure tools. Yet in many cases we still rely on what is called the auditory modality – that means the person's ability to listen and understand through sound rather than through pictures (visual) or through experience (kinaesthetic). Most of the research indicates that children with dyslexia have a phonological difficulty, which means that they have difficulty with sounds. They find it difficult to remember the sound combinations and the sequence of sounds that make up a word. Listening may therefore not be the easiest means of acquiring information. Usually it is better if children with dyslexia can see the information to be learned.

Children with dyslexia can have difficulty in remembering information – This can apply to short-term and working memory and means that it can affect the recall of oral instructions, especially if many items are presented at the same time. The short-term, or working, memory can only hold a limited amount of information, but as children and adults with dyslexia can have difficulty in remembering even a limited amount accurately, it is best to provide only one instruction at any one time.

Children with dyslexia can have difficulty in organising information – Whether we are aware of it or not, we always make some attempt to organise new information. We might group new items to be remembered into one category, and when we are recalling information we generally do that in a fairly organised way so that the listener can understand. This can be especially important if we are recalling a sequence of events. Children with dyslexia can have some difficulty in organising information and this can affect both how efficiently information is remembered and how it is presented to others. This can affect their performance in examinations unless some additional support is available.

Children with dyslexia need more time to process information – This can be very characteristic of dyslexia as children and adults with dyslexia will usually take longer to process information because they may take an indirect route to arrive at an answer. This is explained more fully in Chapter 3, but it emphasises the individuality of dyslexia and the often right-hemisphere way of processing information.

Children with dyslexia will usually have difficulties with reading and also spelling and fluency problems in both reading and writing – You will note that the word 'usually' is mentioned here. This is because not every child with dyslexia will have difficulty in reading and spelling. Some children can compensate for a reading difficulty by becoming very adept at using context and tend to read for meaning. These children may still, however, show some of the other characteristics of dyslexia, particularly those aspects that relate to information processing, such as memory and organisation.

Similarly they may have a difficulty in reading but not in spelling, or vice versa, which again emphasises the individual nature of dyslexia where different children can show dyslexic characteristics to a different degree.

Recognising the presence of dyslexia can, in some circumstances, be quite difficult and the characteristics can easily be mistaken for other conditions. Many children who do not have dyslexia can show similar characteristics. The child with dyslexia, however, usually shows a number of the characteristics shown in Table 1.1 and will often have difficulty with reading, spelling and expressive writing. The performances in these areas can also show a discrepancy with the dyslexic child's other abilities. For example, poor reading performances can contrast with good understanding and problem-solving skills when discussing topics orally.

Although the degree of dyslexia can differ, the indicators are usually fairly constant, but these can also depend on the age of the child. It is also possible to note some of the indicators of dyslexia before the child attends school – that is, before he or she begins to learn to read.

Table 1.1   Continuum of characteristics of dyslexia

Pre-school (characteristics)	Early school years (characteristics)	Persistent difficulties (characteristics)
Reading	*Reading*	*Reading*
• Difficulty in remembering nursery rhymes • May confuse words that sound similar such as boat and bought • May get the sequence of sounds mixed up; e.g. if his name is 'Jonathan', he may say 'Jothanan'	• Difficulty in recognising sounds, combinations of letters that make up sounds such as 'ph' and 'th', and remembering these and using them in a word such as 'thing' and 'elephant' • Getting the sounds and the letters in words out of sequence such as elephant can be read as 'ephelant' • Substitution of words when reading aloud, for example saying 'car' for 'bus' • Continuing difficulty with rhyming and in particular remembering the sequence of the rhyme	• Reading speed tends to be slow and hesitant • Reluctance to read for pleasure • Low self-esteem • Reluctance to read aloud

Continues

Table 1.1 *Continues*

Pre-school (characteristics)	Early school years (characteristics)	Persistent difficulties (characteristics)
Coordination	*Coordination*	*Coordination*
• Can appear clumsy • May have poor pencil grip • Can have difficulty with some fine motor tasks such as threading beads • Can have difficulty in tying shoelaces	• Can have difficulty in some subjects like physical education that require some coordination and often following instructions • May have a difficulty with tying shoelaces and may appear dishevelled at times; may bump into furniture in the classroom, trip and fall more frequently than would be expected	• General clumsiness • Difficulty with eye–hand coordination • Difficulty with some sporting activities
Reaction time	*Reaction time*	*Reaction time*
• May have a vacant expression when asked to do something because he needs time to understand and process the information	• May take longer than expected to respond to tasks • May allow others to take the lead in some tasks	• Will need extra time to complete tasks and for examinations
Memory – short term and long term	*Memory – short term and long term*	*Memory – short term and long term*
• May have difficulty in remembering some information such as age, address and names of friends and relatives • May have difficulty in remembering simple instructions	• Will have difficulty remembering lists of information and dates including date of birth • May have difficulty in remembering homework and difficulty in remembering days of week and days of any after-school clubs	• May show signs of poor long-term memory; difficulty revising for examinations • May have difficulty remembering homework • May have difficulty remembering timetable

Pre-school (characteristics)	Early school years (characteristics)	Persistent difficulties (characteristics)
Spelling	*Spelling*	*Spelling*
• May have difficulty spelling own name	• May make phonological (sound) errors in spelling, for example 'f' for 'ph' • Letters out of sequence • Inconsistent use of some letters with similar sounds such as 's' and 'z' • May spell a word correctly one day but not the next day	• Difficulty remembering spelling rules • Difficulty with word endings, for example using 'ie' for 'y' • Confusion or omission of vowels • May need to rely heavily on computer spell-checker
Writing	*Writing*	*Writing*
• Poor pencil grip • Difficulty with colouring in drawings	• Writing can be slow and deliberate lacking in any fluency speed • Inconsistent use of capital and small letters • May be reluctant to write • Sometimes unusual or awkward pencil grip • May not sit comfortably when writing	• Inconsistent writing style • May have fatigue when writing for long spells
Organisation	*Organisation*	*Organisation*
• Will forget where they put items	• It is likely that their school bag will be untidy • May lose things easily, including important items like homework notebook • May have difficulty in preparing in advance for subjects like physical education or art when they need to bring additional clothes or materials	• Inefficient organisational strategies when learning new material • Poor organisation of timetable, materials equipment and items needed for learning

Continues

Table 1.1 *Continues*

Pre-school (characteristics)	Early school years (characteristics)	Persistent difficulties (characteristics)
Speech and language	*Speech and language*	*Speech and language*
• May be late in developing speech	• Articulation can be quite poor • Difficulty blending sounds into words • Can have a difficulty in remembering the names and words for some everyday items	• May speak in a jumbled disorganised manner • May speak in a hurried manner • May not be very clear in speech

Finding out

Parents may want to access different types of information depending on the circumstances, the age of their son/daughter, the degree of dyslexia and the nature of the characteristics of dyslexia that have been identified. For example, some parents may want to know about (a) the causes of dyslexia, (b) what the future holds for their dyslexic son or daughter, (c) what the school can do and how long it will take their child to catch up, and (d) what they, as parents, can do to help. Others may want to find out about complementary and alternative intervention techniques that may be available outwith the school. Irrespective of the information required, it is important that accurate and reliable sources are available. There are many websites with information on dyslexia and reports on new and innovative therapies, but it is best to seek advice from the school or other professionals (see also Chapter 9). Professionals, with experience of dyslexia, can put any interventions in the context of your child's dyslexic profile and ensure that whatever is done outwith school is complementary and consistent with the overall educational aims and methods used in school. This is not to suggest that the school has always the right answers and the information and resources necessary for dealing with dyslexia, but that all groups involved with the child need to collaborate and work together. Multidisciplinary meetings, if appropriate, can be very beneficial in ensuring shared knowledge and collaboration.

Dyslexia: confusion and clarity

There are many misconceptions about dyslexia and many areas of misunderstanding. Communication between all concerned with the educational, social and personal development of children with dyslexia is vitally important as this can help to avoid any misunderstandings and ensure that all those involved with dyslexic children are working together.

What are these misconceptions and why do they arise? To answer this question it is perhaps useful to look at how professionals define dyslexia.

Understanding dyslexia

There are three main factors that can help in the understanding and definition of dyslexia. These relate to:

- Neurological/brain
- Cognitive/learning
- Educational/environment/learning experiences.

Neurological/brain

There is now considerable evidence that there is a neurological basis to dyslexia. This means that the brain structure and the neural connections needed for processing information may develop differently in dyslexic children. This does not necessarily imply a deficit, but rather a difference. Dyslexic children and adults have no less potential for learning than children who are not dyslexic, but will learn differently and find some types of processing tasks, such as those involving print and language, more challenging. This point will also be developed in more detail in the chapter on learning (Chapter 3).

The hemispheres

There are two hemispheres in the brain – the left and the right – and generally speaking each hemisphere is more adept at processing certain

Left hemisphere	Right hemisphere
● Handwriting	● Mathematical computation
● Language	● Spatial awareness
● Reading	● Shapes and patterns
● Phonics	● Colour sensitivity
● Locating details and facts	● Singing and music
● Talking and reciting	● Art expression
● Following directions	● Creativity
● Listening	● Visualisation
● Auditory association	● Feelings and emotions

Figure 1.1   Skills usually associated with the hemispheres

types of information (see Figure 1.1) Generally, the left hemisphere processes language and the small details of information, such as print. This means that the left hemisphere is important for decoding the tasks that are necessary for accurate reading.

The right hemisphere tends to process information that incorporates a more holistic stimuli, and would involve the processing of pictures and other types of visual information. As a rule, the right hemisphere also deals with comprehension and some of the aesthetic aspects, such as art and music. The works of Galaburda (1993a, 1993b), West (1991/1997) and many others have highlighted that children and adults with dyslexia usually have a right-hemisphere processing preference or style. Some neuropsychologists, such as Dirk Bakker in Holland, have related this to reading and have suggested that right-hemisphere individuals can become 'sloppy' readers, but may have good comprehension skills (Robertson & Bakker, 2002).

Phonological skills

While children with dyslexia can often show skills in right-hemisphere processing, they may have difficulty in processing information using the left hemisphere. The skills necessary for accurate reading tend to be left-hemisphere skills, such as the skills needed to discriminate different sounds in words. These skills are called 'phonological skills' and are essential for identifying the cluster of letters that make certain sounds, such as 'ough' as in 'tough' and 'ight' as in 'right'. It is now widely accepted that children with dyslexia have a weakness in phonological skills and this – especially in young readers – will certainly affect their ability to read fluently. There is, however, evidence that if intervention to teach phonological skills takes place at an early age, the acquisition of literacy can become more accessible.

Implications

The implications of the above is that children and adults with dyslexia can have many strengths, as well as the more obvious difficulties – and especially those associated with literacy. It also means that children with dyslexia will learn differently and this will therefore have implications for teaching in the classroom and for examinations.

Visual aspects

There is also evidence to suggest that some children with dyslexia may, in fact, have a visual processing difficulty or, indeed, can have both visual and phonological difficulties. In this research, Professor John Stein from the University of Oxford in the UK (Stein, 2004), has made considerable breakthroughs in this area, especially in relation to the group of cells in the visual cortex known as the magnocellular system. These cells, which control eye movements and visual acuity when the eyes are in motion, do not seem to operate appropriately in the sample of dyslexic children studied by Stein and colleagues. This can affect reading accuracy and fluency and is called the Magnocellular Deficit Hypothesis. The neural pathways of the visual system can be divided on anatomical bases into two streams: the *parvocellular* (P) and *magnocellular* (M) systems, which are sensitive to different types of stimuli in different ways. The parvocellular system seems to respond to slowly changing (low-frequency) information, to more detailed stimuli (i.e. higher frequencies) and to colour. The magno-cellular system, on the other hand, is more sensitive to gross (lower-frequency), rapidly changing (high-frequency) or moving information. Dr John Everatt from the University of Surrey (Everatt, 2002) reports on research relating to dyslexic children's poor performance on tasks assessing the functioning of the magnocellular pathway and indicates that research studies have found abnormal cell size and organisation in magnocellular layers of the visual system of individuals with reading disabilities.

The encouraging point is that visual-processing difficulties can be made less problematic with various interventions and accommodations such as the use of coloured overlays and coloured paper as well as tracking magnifiers that cover up all the words on a page except those that are to be read.

Motor control

This refers to coordination, movement and balance. There are a number of researchers working in this area and there are also a number of assessment and intervention strategies that have been developed to identify and deal with movement difficulties (for further information on this, see Portwood, 2001, and McIntyre, 2001). Difficulties with motor development itself can be placed on a continuum from mild to severe, and there may be different causes for the difficulties experienced within this continuum. Angela Fawcett and Rod Nicolson from the University of Sheffield in the UK (Fawcett & Nicolson, 2004) developed and advanced the Cerebellar Deficit Hypothesis. This implies that children with dyslexia show evidence of immaturity in the development of the cerebellum. The cerebellum has a number of important functions, but is usually associated with motor control, movement and balance. It also seems to link with other key processing elements such as processing speed, phonological awareness and visual processing. One of the items in the Dyslexia Screening Test (Fawcett & Nicolson, 1996) relates to balance and postural stability.

The implications of this is that often these difficulties can interfere with other processing activities and affect the development of literacy skills. Motor difficulties can range from gross motor difficulties that affect walking, running and posture – with the child showing obvious signs of clumsiness – to difficulties associated with fine motor control that can affect pencil grip and handwriting in general.

Genetic factors

One of the most significant developments in recent years has occurred in the area of genetics. It has long been suspected that a family trait is associated with dyslexia, and studies in the field of genetics have shown that this is certainly the case.

A study by Gilger et al. (1991) in the USA estimates that the risk of a son being dyslexic if he has a dyslexic father is about 40%; and Castles et al. (1999) found a strong heritability element among 'phonological dyslexics' – that is, dyslexic children who have a difficulty with the sounds of words. There have also been studies attempting to identify the actual chromosomes and specific genes that are responsible for dyslexia, and gene markers for dyslexia have been found in chromosome 6 (Fisher et al., 1999). This, and similar studies, indicate the presence of a possible site for 'dyslexic genes' in chromosome 6 and significantly they may be in the same region as the genes implicated in autoimmune diseases. Ailments associated with the autoimmune system, such as asthma, hay fever and allergies, have been reported to show a high level of association with dyslexia (Snowling, 2000).

The important aspect for parents, and teachers, in relation to these genetic studies is that they may lead to earlier identification and this, in turn, can make early intervention more relevant and more successful.

Cognitive/learning

Cognition means 'thinking' and cognitive aspects relate to the processing system in the brain that deals with information of any kind – including how we understand, store in memory and recall information. This obviously is an important aspect of learning and it is necessary to use our cognitive processes efficiently if learning is to be thorough and effective. There is considerable evidence that children and adults with dyslexia do not use their cognitive processes efficiently, and this cannot only result in poor memory and slow processing speed but they may also take longer to learn some types of information and skill. With the use of effective strategies, and effective teaching, some of the negative effects of these factors can be minimised. Children with dyslexia may always have a dyslexic processing style, but with self-knowledge and self-sufficiency in learning they can use their processing style to their advantage. This will be developed in Chapter 3. Some of the 'cognitive' aspects that can be challenging for children with dyslexia are described in Table 1.2.

Table 1.2 Difficulties, affect and intervention

Cognitive difficulties	Affect on child	Intervention
Phonological awareness	Will affect decoding print and unknown words that cannot be read visually will be difficult	Early intervention best, teach nursery rhymes, games involving words, and the sounds of letters and letter combinations
Short-term memory	Will make it difficult to store information for a short period; such as instructions	Memory games, use of mnemonics and other visual strategies
Working memory	Will make it difficult to store more than one item in short-term memory and to hold information while carrying out a task such as in mental arithmetic	Only give one instruction at a time. Ensure one item is understood and can be recalled before moving on to the next
Naming and labelling	May forget the names of everyday items or may take longer to recall them	Reinforce the use of labels and names. Label items if necessary but always use the name of items
Processing speed	Take longer period of time to learn new information and may lose the track of a problem because it takes a long time to process	Provide a structure to problems that can show the steps to be taken. Encourage small steps and monitor progress in each step
Organisation	Will find it difficult to locate information and locate items	Strategies such as grouping similar things together. Routine and the use of colour for different items can help

Cognitive difficulties	Affect on child	Intervention
Automaticity	This means that learning will take longer to be automatic that is done without thinking how it is done	Over-learning and reinforcement. The use of a skill or new word will help to achieve automaticity

Educational/environment/learning experiences

It is important that, as a parent, you are aware of the educational implications and educational experiences with which your child is provided. It is also important that parents and the school communicate effectively and work collaboratively.

Educational factors that are important include the learning environment and an acknowledgement of the child's particular learning style. The learning environment means the size of school, class size, type of classroom layout and the quality of the learning experiences provided to the child. There is no right or wrong method in relation to the learning environment as children with dyslexia may have different preferences from each other. When working at home, however, a quiet environment will usually be best, but only for short periods. Working in a very quiet environment for too long may actually prove distracting for the child, and some background music may help to release the tension from a very quiet room. Ideally the working environment should include some time in a quiet room, some time with background music and some time with others in a busier type of environment.

It is important to be aware of the child's learning style. Although many children with dyslexia use a right-hemisphere approach to learning they can all show specific differences and each child will have a particular preference and style for learning. Parents and teachers should acknowledge the importance of learning styles. This can help children with dyslexia to become aware of their learning style, so that when they are learning independently at school, or when they leave school, they can do so using their own style. There is evidence to suggest that if children are aware, and able to use their own learning style, they will be more effective learners.

Characteristics of dyslexia: comment

While parents may receive some information on the characteristics of dyslexia, many still feel confused particularly when they read, or hear about, conflicting views on dyslexia. As was indicated earlier in this chapter, there are many characteristics of dyslexia and perhaps this is how the confusion arises. Not every child with dyslexia will display all of the characteristics; some may have only the motor/visual perceptual characteristics and, therefore, will respond to different intervention than those dyslexic children who have a pronounced phonological difficulty. It is for that reason that a full and comprehensive assessment is essential.

Definition of dyslexia

This introductory chapter includes a definition of dyslexia (p. 17). It is worth noting that many definitions are used by governments, voluntary and professional organisations, education authorities and school districts throughout the world. Many of these, although they may appear different and emphasise different aspects, often describe the same type of factors.

Key points in a definition

- Processing difference
- Can affect cognitive areas
- May be visual and phonological difficulties
- Discrepancy in performances in different areas of learning
- Important that individual differences and learning styles are considered
- Important to recognise the importance of the learning and work context

These points can be noted in the following definition, but in addition to these points some definitions mention the fact that dyslexia often has a neurological cause and/or a genetic trait. Others mention the need for specific teaching approaches and occasionally list specific aspects such as memory, organisation and processing speed.

I have used the following definition in an accompanying book on dyslexia for teachers.

> Dyslexia is a processing difference experienced by people of all ages, often characterised by difficulties in literacy, it can affect other cognitive areas such as memory, speed of processing, time management, co-ordination and directional aspects. There may be visual and phonological difficulties and there is usually some discrepancy in performances in different areas of learning. It is important that the individual differences and learning styles are acknowledged since these will effect outcomes of learning and assessment. It is also important to consider the learning and work context as the nature of the difficulties associated with dyslexia may well be more pronounced in some learning situations.
>
> (Reid, 2003)

Issues parents have to deal with

There are many issues that parents have to deal with from the time they suspect their son or daughter may have dyslexia. These issues can cause some confusion, and this confusion can be felt in a number of different ways. These will be discussed below and will also be dealt with in more detail in subsequent chapters. Some of these issues are:

- Obtaining an assessment
- Communication
- Advice and support.

Obtaining an assessment

For many parents, obtaining an assessment can be a confusing and anxious process. Dyslexia is one of the few educational needs where private independent assessments are as commonplace as school administered assessments. This situation is applicable across the globe. In fact in many countries it is the shortage of experienced and qualified personnel who can conduct an assessment that provides difficulties for parents, and many parents have travelled considerable distances to obtain an appropriate assessment. Many school districts and education authorities now have qualified teachers who can provide insights into the educational needs of the child and nature of the child's difficulties. Often, however, an educational psychologist has to make the final diagnosis and parents may have to wait some time for this unless they engage an independent psychologist for a private assessment. While not everyone can afford a private assessment, it can provide the parents with information relating to their child's cognitive profile and specifically in relation to dyslexia. Every attempt in the first instance, however, should be made to obtain this type of assessment from the school.

Communication

Irrespective of whether the assessment is obtained independent of the school, it is vital that parents and school work together. Constructive communication is the key to a successful outcome. If communication between home and school breaks down, the child may receive conflicting and confusing messages in relation to his or her dyslexia, and this can be detrimental in both the short and the long term.

Communication can be in the form of a home/school notebook which can detail the work done that day or week at school and suggest how the parents may follow this up at home. Naturally, personal communication is preferable and contact should be made as early as possible in the school term. It should be noted, however, that teachers and management are normally quite busy in the first few weeks of term, but at least some contact, even briefly, can be made and a longer appointment can be arranged for a later date.

It is important that parents acknowledge the school's aims, but they are entitled to be involved in any individual educational plan for their child. This is important as such a plan should have follow-up home activities. This is extremely crucial for children with dyslexia, as in order to achieve automaticity they need overlearning and this can be carried out at home as well as school. Thus a new word learned at school can be reinforced at home through discussion – for example, if the child has just learned the word group that uses the 'ch' ending, as in watch, catch and batch, this can be noted by parents and followed up when opportunities present themselves. It is through practice and reinforcement that children with dyslexia will achieve automaticity, and this emphasises why a consistent approach and communication between home and school is vital.

Some children with dyslexia can have difficulty when they move from one school to another. This, of course, can arise if parents move to another area and at the point of transfer from primary to secondary school. Sometimes it can be difficult for children with dyslexia to fit into a new school setting and they often need a period of readjustment. They have to become aware of the conventions and routine of the class and the school. Expectations of children can vary from school to school and the routines can also vary. Additionally, some school buildings – especially larger schools – may have a confusing layout and this can also introduce difficulties as children with dyslexia can often have spatial problems and difficulty in finding their way around the school. It is advisable, therefore, that parents make contact with the school as early as possible in the term, especially if there has been a change of teacher or a change of school. This will also help the parents to become aware of the norms and expectations of the class and the teachers' expectations of the children. The parents may have to reinforce this at home to ensure that the children understand the school procedure, and a consistent message should always be presented between home and school.

Advice and support

When parents find out that their son or daughter has dyslexia, it is quite natural that they will want to find out something about the problem and will seek advice from various sources. There are a number of advisory sources, but it is probably best to seek advice from the most local source. Much depends on the education provision and the level of support that schools in your area offer to dyslexic children. Most countries have national organisations that can offer advice, such as the British Dyslexia Association in the UK, the International Dyslexia

Association (IDA) in the USA and the European Dyslexia Association in European countries. There is also an organisation called SPELD in New Zealand and Australia and all these organisations have local branches. Details of these and other organisations, as well as websites dedicated to supporting parents, can be found in Chapter 9 of this book.

These organisations will be able to offer advice on your children's needs and there are some general principles that parents, and indeed schools, should follow. In the UK, for example, many of these suggestions are highlighted in the criteria disseminated by the British Dyslexia Association in collaboration with teachers, psychologists and school management in setting standards that are now known as criteria for 'dyslexia-friendly schools'. In the USA, the IDA also publish guidelines and advice on their website and in the members' journal, *Perspectives*.

Neil Mackay in the UK (Mackay, 2004) suggests that 'dyslexia-friendly' equals 'learning friendly' and that every school should seek to become dyslexia-friendly for that reason. He provides the following scenario:

Imagine a school that recognises that all children learn in different ways and teachers harness the power of learning styles and learning preferences to optimise teaching and learning. In this school teachers also recognise that many apparent learning **difficulties** can often be explained as learning **differences** that respond to changes in methods, materials and approaches. Also many of the special educational needs that formerly occupied the attention of class/subject teachers and specialist teachers are now seen as ordinary learning needs that are dealt with through the differentiated curriculum plan. As a result the school is writing far fewer Individual Education Plans (IEPs): but those that are written are of high quality, are very carefully monitored and evaluated to actively direct and inform the way children are taught in mainstream settings.

The school is particularly aware of the needs of the growing numbers of non-traditional learners who do not function well in some learning environments and who often think faster than they read, write, spell or do number work. An interesting aspect of this school is the calm, confident way in which all children approach their learning. Even the most vulnerable learners are set up to succeed because they are effectively working within their comfort zone for much of the time and operating from a secure platform of strength and competence.

Mackay goes on to suggest

that this type of school should see parents as partners and such schools will enjoy the trust of parents and will be able to provide evidence of this trust in the form of written comments at review, letters of thanks/support and in the way the parents of dyslexic children are involved in the life of the school. A key element in establishing parental trust is the speed with which a school responds to concerns raised and the thoroughness with which dialogue is initiated and maintained.

(Adapted from Mackay, 2004)

This is the type of school that would reduce the anxiety of parents of children with dyslexia. One of the key aspects of this is that dyslexia is not necessarily seen as a disability, but as a difference and it is up to the school to ensure that they can accommodate the differences shown by children with dyslexia.

The Northern Ireland *Task Group Report on Dyslexia* (Northern Ireland Education Dept, 2002), which reported in April 2002, suggested that school ethos, and how parents of children with dyslexia were incorporated into that ethos, is an important element in developing satisfactory links between home and school.

Many of the points made above in Mackay's ideal school are, in fact, encapsulated in page 55 of the Northern Ireland report in which the Task Group endorsed the following as good practice:

- Children's differences/difficulties are identified and addressed at an early stage to avoid the consequence of frustration and failure.
- They understand their learning differences/difficulties and feel supported by adults who understand them.
- They are catered for in a pastoral care system that is proactive in ensuring their emotional well-being.
- They feel free to discuss their differences/difficulties with understanding teachers/support staff.
- Their peers are understanding of their learning differences and are sympathetic towards them.
- They have opportunity to share mutual support with other children who have similar difficulties.
- Their parents are informed partners with the school in supporting them emotionally and educationally.

- They have opportunities to build self-esteem and self-confidence through success and achievement in a well-managed and well-balanced curricular programme.
- They are encouraged to play a full part in the life of the school.

This latter point, that 'they are encouraged to play a full part in the life of the school', is crucial, and one of the ways of developing that practice is to provide some opportunities for success within the curriculum. One of the most appropriate ways of doing this is to ensure that all children with dyslexia have access to the curriculum. Yet, many can be deprived such access. For example, parents may be encouraged to agree that their son or daughter omits modern languages from the timetable, and although it may be a welcome suggestion when the young person is overburdened with homework, and learning is progressing at a slow pace, it should **not** be necessary. In their book, Margaret Crombie and Elke Schneider (Crombie & Schneider, 2003) have shown how schools and colleges can differentiate to ensure that all dyslexic children have access to modern languages. It is important, therefore, that any decisions that are made in relation to the child's subject choice are shared decisions made in collaboration between parents and the school.

Crombie and Schneider (2003) suggest that 'we owe it to our pupils to give them opportunities which will help them realise their potential in a foreign language environment'. They stress, for example, that teachers of foreign languages need to provide a learning atmosphere in which language patterns are made explicit through dialogue between students and teachers. In these dialogues, students practise verbalising their thinking processes and knowledge in the foreign language regarding pronunciation, grammar, vocabulary, spelling, speaking and writing paradigms, as well as cultural components. They practise thinking out loud to identify and solve language problems, such as spelling errors, reading errors or comprehension difficulties.

Although this is an example aimed at teachers, it is included in this book as a source of encouragement and support to parents. It indicates that even in demanding subjects such as modern languages, which can be very challenging for children with dyslexia, much can still be done. This has implications for teachers and for curriculum development. It also has implications for parents to ensure that their children's needs are met. There are many misconceptions about dyslexia, and particularly in relation to modern foreign languages, such as the view indicated above that language studies for children with dyslexia are inappropriate. This example, and the work of Crombie and Schneider and many others, indicate that this is not necessarily an accurate view, yet it is one that is prevalent. It not only highlights the importance of seeking out and receiving appropriate and accurate advice, but also highlights the need to seek advice from different sources. Advice should be sought in a positive way but, unfortunately, in many cases parents are often in despair before they seek advice, and it is, in fact, this despair that prompts them to look for advice. It is always best to get advice as early as possible. In researching for this book, I administered a questionnaire to parents via my home page on the world wide web and I remember one response in particular. One of the questions that parents were asked was to list the supports that were available to them. One despondent parent firmly answered 'None'. I am sure this is exactly how this parent felt, but it is unfortunate that with the widespread knowledge of dyslexia that is around, and the abundance of support sources available, some parents still feel totally unsupported.

Summary

This chapter has provided an introduction to dyslexia for parents and identified some of the main issues with which parents have to deal. It is also important that parents have a good understanding of what dyslexia is and how to seek advice that may help them to support their dyslexic child at home. The chapter therefore provides an overview of the characteristics of dyslexia and explains some of the theoretical background relating to these characteristics. The chapter also attempts to clarify some of the confusions and misconceptions that surround dyslexia. Children with dyslexia have the potential to achieve a great deal at school and even subjects that can be quite demanding, such as modern languages, should not be outwith the reach of such children.

Supporting and helping dyslexic children at home is a very important issue, and one that understandably parents ask about. Some suggestions are made here concerning parental help at home, and these are followed up in more detail in Chapter 3. One of the important points relates to communication, and particularly communication with the school. This is emphasised strongly in this chapter, and later chapters will contain suggestions on how this can be achieved. The chapter ends on a positive note by suggesting that, despite the anxieties and difficulties faced by parents and children, there have been considerable developments in schools in awareness of, and in support for, children with dyslexia. There is a great deal of support available, and no parent of a child with dyslexia should feel isolated.

Chapter 2

Identification and assessment: guidance for parents

It is not beyond most teachers, and indeed many parents, to identify or suspect that a child has dyslexia. The characteristics of dyslexia are fairly well known and parents can spot many of these characteristics. Some of the most common of these are described in Figure 2.1.

In addition, parents can be on the alert if there is a history of dyslexia in the family. As indicated in the previous chapter, there is now strong evidence to suggest that dyslexia is inherited, although there is likely to be a number of genes and genetic permutations responsible for dyslexia. Nevertheless, the presence of dyslexia in either the immediate or extended family can be an important factor in early identification.

The importance of assessment

Once parents, or teachers, have identified that the child may have some, or all, of the characteristics of dyslexia, it is important to obtain a full and comprehensive assessment. One of the questions parents often ask is at what age should such an assessment take place. This is quite tricky because some of the characteristics of dyslexia can be noted in the

The child shows difficulty with some, or all, of the following:

- Sequencing numbers or letters in the right order
- Following instructions and getting instructions confused
- Telling or re-telling a story in the correct sequence
- Fine motor skills, such as pencil control and difficulty tying shoelaces
- Gross motor difficulties, such as clumsiness
- Left/right confusion
- Confusing some common sounds
- Remembering nursery rhymes
- Remembering days of week in sequence
- Remembering numbers and possibly shapes of objects
- Poor concentration with some activities, especially those activities that require concentrated attention
- Possible speech difficulties, has difficulty pronouncing some multisyllabic words
- Adding new words to his or her vocabulary
- Learning the alphabet

Figure 2.1 Characteristics of dyslexia

normal development of young children. But if the child has not made the expected progress throughout the first year of school, then at that point a formal assessment should be considered. Such an assessment can identify some possible reasons for the lack of progress as well as locate areas of strength and weakness. An assessment should also lead to a set of recommendations and the results may suggest a further specialist assessment, such as that from an optometrist, or a speech or occupational therapist.

Some professionals hold the view that it can be counter-productive for a formal assessment for dyslexia to place while the child is still very young. While there are some risks attached to this, such as mis-diagnosis or unnecessary or premature labelling, it does seem that the advantages of early assessment and obtaining a comprehensive profile of the child's cognitive strengths and weaknesses can outweigh any possible disadvantages.

Research in dyslexia and early intervention (Crombie et al., 2004) clearly indicates the advantages of early identification and indicates that early intervention will be more successful if a clear profile of the child's difficulties and strengths are available.

Early screening

Reid Lyon (1998), in discussing the situation in the USA, made the following comment:

> We have learned that for 90% to 95% of poor readers, prevention and early intervention programs that combine instruction in phoneme awareness, phonics, fluency development, and reading comprehension strategies, provided by well-trained teachers, can increase reading skills to average reading levels. However, we have also learned that if we delay intervention until nine-years-of-age (the time that most children with reading difficulties receive services), approximately 75% of the children will continue to have difficulties learning to read throughout high school.

This emphasises the importance of early identification and the recognition of appropriate early intervention. Many schools do have well-developed policies for the early years, but children with dyslexia will usually require additional considerations and perhaps more intensive input such as that briefly described above by Reid Lyon (Reid Lyon, 1998; Reid Lyon et al., 2004).

There are some early screening tests for dyslexia that have been standardised in larger samples of populations. Some of the checklists that are fairly widely available may not have undergone such rigorous standardisation. In relation to the pre-school period there are three tests that are particularly suitable and can be administered by pre-school teaching staff. These are the Dyslexia Early Screening Test (DEST; Fawcett & Nicolson, 1997), the Dyslexia Pre-School Early Screening Test (PREST; Fawcett et al., 2001) and the computerised screening program called CoPS (Computerised Cognitive Screening; Singleton, 1996). All three tests are well standardised. The DEST and PREST consist of series of sub-tests that investigate areas of potential importance in identifying dyslexia, such as knowledge of sounds, coordination, memory and processing speed. The CoPS program constitutes a user-friendly package that provides a graphic report and printout of results. The CoPS suite has undergone extensive piloting and has also been converted to several languages. CoPS is now used in over 3,500 primary schools in the UK and elsewhere in the world (Singleton, 2002). There is also the CoPS baseline assessment (Singleton et al., 1999).

The above tests can provide useful information that can inform a diagnosis by a professional person. It is important, however, that parents have some understanding of what these tests look for and why they are seen by many professionals in different countries as being suitable for early diagnosis.

The Dyslexia Early Screening Test – This test looks for difficulties in short-term memory, balance, coordination, spelling, speed of processing, reading accuracy, reading fluency and phonological processing.

PREST – This test can screen children aged 3 years 6 months to 4 years 5 months. PREST 1: consists of rapid naming, beads threading and paper cutting, digits and letters, repetition, shape copying and spatial memory. The PREST is intended to screen all children and the PREST 2 those children with an 'at risk' score in the PREST 1. The sub-tests in PREST 2 are balance, phonological discrimination, digit-span, rhyming, sound order and form matching.

Lucid CoPS Cognitive Profile System – This consists of activities comprising up to nine games, each with graphic and cartoon characters. As the child plays the games the computer records his or her cognitive skills. These include short-term memory, phonological awareness, auditory and colour discrimination.

There is also a test called the Lucid Rapid Dyslexia Screening Test which is available for children aged 4–15. It comprises three assessment modules, all testing skills that can relate to dyslexia such as phonological awareness. (Details are available from www.lucid-research.com.)

Special Needs Assessment Profile

The Special Needs Assessment Profile (SNAP; Weedon & Reid, 2003) is a computer-aided diagnostic assessment and profiling package that makes it possible to track each child's own profile on to an overall matrix providing information on learning, behavioural and other difficulties. From this, clusters and patterns of weaknesses and strengths help to identify the core features of a child's difficulties – visual, dyslexic, dyspraxic, phonological, attentional or any other of the 15 key deficits targeted in SNAP. This can suggest a diagnosis that points the way forward for a teaching programme for an individual child. SNAP involves four steps:

- Step 1 *(Pupil Assessment Pack)*: Structured questionnaire checklists for completion by class teachers and parents give an initial 'outline map' of the child's difficulties.
- Step 2 *(CD-ROM)*: The learning support staff charts the child's difficulties, using the CD-ROM to identify patterns and target any further diagnostic follow-up assessments to be carried out at Step 3.
- Step 3 *(User's Kit)*: Focused assessments from a photo-copiable resource bank of quick diagnostic 'probes' yield a detailed and textured understanding of the child's difficulties.
- Step 4 *(CD-ROM)*: The computer-generated profile yields specific guidance on support (including personalised information sheets for parents) and practical follow-up.

The kit helps to facilitate the collaboration between different groups of professionals and between professionals and parents, which is extremely vital in order to obtain a full picture of a student's abilities and difficulties. There is a dedicated website that can be accessed by anyone and contains a number of ideas on teaching, and for the home, to cover difficulties associated with 15 different specific learning difficulties.

The website is www.SNAPassessment.com.

Checklists

It is possible for parents to be presented with a checklist that may indicate a number of dyslexic characteristics. There are many variations of checklists for identifying dyslexia and some are easily accessible from web pages. Checklists, however, need to be treated with considerable caution. They are not, in any form, a definitive diagnosis of dyslexia and can, in fact, be of fairly limited value, except perhaps for a preliminary screening before a more detailed assessment. Nevertheless, checklists usually provide a range of information that may produce a picture of your child's strengths and weaknesses. Even these can still be very limited and are no substitute for a comprehensive educational-based assessment looking at the classroom environment, the curriculum as well as the learner's strengths and weaknesses. Checklists can then be used to monitor progress.

Who assesses?

If you, or your child's teacher, suspect that there is a possibility of dyslexia, then it is important to obtain a full assessment. The procedures for obtaining this vary from country to country, and can even vary considerably within a country. Usually, however, educational psychologists are the group of professionals who can provide a full diagnosis and accompanying learning profile from which recommendations for teaching and learning can be made. Increasingly, however, assessments can also be performed in many countries by specialist teachers who have undergone recognised courses in dyslexia. It should also be noted that in some countries there can be a requirement that an assessment by an educational psychologist is carried out before any special provision or arrangements can be made.

Nevertheless, teacher assessments are vitally important and these can often relate more directly to the curriculum and the day-to-day learning difficulties and strengths of the child than a diagnosis obtained by a professional who may have no previous working knowledge of the child. Naturally it is better for professionals to work together in a collaborative manner as each will have something useful to contribute to the assessment. The message here is that everyone – psychologists, teachers, parents and, when appropriate, other professionals, such as occupational therapists, speech and language therapists and medical personnel – may each have a function to play in an assessment. Table 2.1 highlights the function of each professional who can be involved in the assessment process.

Role of professionals

Table 2.1 Role of professionals

Professional	Function	Access
Educational psychologist	Can administer intelligence tests and other restricted tests	Can be through school or privately, but need to ensure that they are properly qualified. See, for example, the *UK Directory of Chartered Psychologists*, which can be consulted in the local public library
Specialist teacher	Can administer specialised tests that have been developed for dyslexia. Will have knowledge of the implications of the results and what action to take	Through school, although some specialist advice and assessment can be provided by voluntary and parent organisations
Class teacher	Can contribute a great deal in terms of information gathered through observation. Will have a detailed knowledge of how the child performs in class and in different types of activities	Through school and parents' evenings
Audiometrician	Deals with hearing and discrimination of sounds	Usually through medical sources but school may also offer advice
Occupational therapist	Deals with movement and can diagnosis specific difficulties in coordination and motor control. Can develop and implement specific exercise-based programs	Usually through medical sources or through school

Continues

Table 2.1 *Continues*

Professional	Function	Access
Optometrist	Deals with visual difficulties, visual acuity, blurring of words when reading and general visual discomfort	Usually privately but school can be first call. Some opticians can provide this service
Speech and language therapist	Deals with all speech difficulties, articulation, comprehension and associated difficulties	Through school or medical sources
Neuropsychologist/ clinical psychologist	Can provide insights if brain or birth trauma and can provide recommendations on programs that do not necessarily have an educational focus	Through medical referral
Occupational psychologist	Can provide guidance on work-based difficulties and recommendations and guidance on career potential and support	Through employment agencies/employer

It can be noted from Table 2.1 that a number of different professionals can have some form of input at some stage in the child's development – depending on the type of difficulty and the situation. It is always best to seek advice on this from the school, if the child is of school age, or from the family doctor if the child is pre-school. Most professionals, however, can be accessed privately and independently, although this can be expensive. If this route is to be taken, it is best to obtain a recommendation either from someone who has used the service before or from a recognised association to which the professional may be affiliated. Below are some details of the roles of various professionals who can be involved in the assessment.

Educational psychologist

Educational psychologists are usually highly qualified professionals in psychology and education who have an understanding of the cognitive processes involved in learning. For that reason they are permitted to use cognitive tests, such as tests that measure intelligence.

The benefit of this in the case of dyslexia is that it can eliminate any other reason for lack of progress in learning or in attainments, such as low IQ. If the child's IQ is found to be low, then the educational priorities will be different from a child who has a higher IQ but is perhaps not performing to his or her best ability. For example, the child with a low IQ may need to focus on language comprehension while a dyslexic child with a higher IQ may require his or her reading accuracy to be prioritised. It should be noted at this point, however, that owing to its focus on language, the IQ test can discriminate against children with dyslexia and the IQ score may not reveal their actual potential.

The IQ test mostly used by the educational psychologist is the Wechsler Intelligence Scale for Children (WISC) (the equivalent test for adults is known as the Wechsler Adult Intelligence Scale: WAIS). These tests, however, can be supplemented by other tests such as the Wechsler Objective Reading Dimensions (WORD) and the Wechsler Objective Language Dimensions (WOLD) and these can correlate with the WISC. The educational psychologist has therefore a battery of tests at his or her disposal.

In many countries it is the educational psychologist who provides a diagnosis, although this is always best acquired through collaboration with the school.

An assessment by an educational psychologist is usually carried out after the school, or the parents, suspect that the child is not making the progress that would be expected, given his or her abilities in other areas. The assessment can also be carried out privately. In the UK, for example, access to an educational psychologist is usually through referral from the school, but private referral can also be made. The British Psychological Society (BPS) publishes a list of chartered psychologists that is updated annually and contains details of the qualifications and the specialisms of every registered member. This directory can usually be referred to in the public library.

Specialist teacher

Many schools have trained and experienced specialist teachers who can carry out a school-based assessment. These teachers will have completed a recognised course of training in dyslexia that should include at least a module on assessment. For example, the British Dyslexia Association awards the accreditation of AMBDA (Associated Member of the British Dyslexia Association) to those teachers who have completed an approved course. (A list of approved courses can be found in the *British Dyslexia Association Handbook*, published annually.)

An assessment conducted by a specialist teacher will provide diagnostic information on the child's level of reading, spelling, writing and number work. Reasons for any lack of progress should be offered and recommendations on teaching programmes and strategies should be made, including what parents can do at home. This aspect will be discussed later in this book.

Class teacher

The class teacher is best placed to obtain first-hand and detailed knowledge of the child's difficulties and strengths as well as the learning preferences and learning style of the child. Many class teachers also have some knowledge of dyslexia, although the extent of this can vary considerably. As a parent you will have a good knowledge of your child and his or her learning pattern and specific difficulties and strengths. It is important to provide this information to the teacher, which further underlines the benefit of good communication with the school.

Role of parents in the assessment

Most schools now accept, or at least should accept, that parents have a key role to play in the assessment process. In fact some schools and educational authorities go further, as was seen in the area of Fife in Scotland when they produced a policy on dyslexia called Partnership: Professionals, Parents and Pupils (Fife Education Authority, 1996). This emphasises the key role that parents of children with dyslexia can play in collaboration with schools.

Parental participation in the assessment

Before an assessment takes place, parents need to ensure that the school is informed of the following:

1. Early pre-school development.
2. The age at which key milestones were reached since birth, e.g. when the child started talking and walking.
3. Any reasons why the parents feel that their child may have dyslexia.
4. Any other reason for possible difficulty in learning, such as problems at birth.
5. Home factors such as behaviour, interest in learning and the things that are motivating.

The assessment

A formal assessment can be a daunting process for both the child and the parents and it is important that the potential for this is minimised. The child should be prepared for the assessment. The actual word 'assessment', however, need not be used as this in itself may induce stress. There are a number of ways of indicating to the child what will happen without using the word 'assessment', and this should minimise any anxiety. Essentially, the tester is engaging in a range of activities with the child to find out how he or she learns and what can be done to help to improve learning. This views assessment as a positive activity, which, of course, it should be.

The parent(s) should try to be available immediately after the assessment to get some initial feedback and to reassure their child on his or her performance. If possible, parents should also speak with the tester before the assessment in order to find out how long the procedure will take and the kind of information the tester is looking for in the assessment.

The person conducting the assessment will need some background information from the parents, particularly relating to any concerns they may have about the development and the behaviours/characteristics of their child. It is helpful to provide some details on how the child behaves at home in terms of his or her social skills, learning pattern and motivation. Much of this information varies, of course, with the age of the child or young adult being tested.

Feedback from the assessment

Feedback following the assessment is extremely important and should ideally involve the class teacher, member of school management team, the parents and, if appropriate, the child. The parents, however, usually want some immediate informal feedback from the assessor. It is also important to give the child some form of informal feedback as soon as possible after the assessment, depending, of course, on the age of the child. The feedback to parents should include the following:

1. Details of the tests administered and the reasons why particular tests were used.
2. The child's test behaviour and motivation. Was the child interested in the test materials and did he or she manage to maintain interest throughout the assessment?
3. How do the results compare to the norm (average). If possible, you can ask to see a graph, or some other visually displayed profile.
4. The implications of the results. This is important as the results should provide information on a diagnosis and, importantly, recommendations for intervention or further assessment.
5. Follow-up assessment and details of any monitoring of progress that will be carried out. This is also important and arrangements and time sequence for monitoring of progress should be indicated. As a parent you should be reassured that the assessment is not the end of the process, but in many cases the beginning. Details of short-, medium- and long-term monitoring should be indicated, although this can best be negotiated with the school.

Understanding assessment reports

There will be a written record of the assessment. Certainly a formal assessment from a psychologist will always be followed up with a written report. A professional report can sometimes be shrouded in technical jargon and this technical vocabulary, if there is no accompanying explanation, can be fairly meaningless to parents. It may be necessary to have a follow-up meeting with the psychologist to discuss the report, but this may not be required if feedback from the assessment is provided as soon as possible after the assessment.

The following example of a specimen assessment report, and the accompanying comments, attempt to provide explanations for the different facets of an assessment report. For ease of clarification the report is divided into the following sections:

1. Background details/reason for assessment
2. Test behaviour/attention and concentration
3. Test used
4. Results and interpretation of results
5. Implications of results
6. Specific recommendations
7. Follow-up assessment/arrangements for monitoring
8. Conclusion/summary.

Interpreting an assessment report

1. Background details

Assessment Report
Confidential

Name of Psychologist/Assessor: ....

Name: ....
School: ....
Address: ....
Date of assessment: ....
Date of report: ....
Date of birth: ....
Age at assessment: .... *years* .... *months*
Background to referral/reasons for the assessment: ....
....

Explanatory comment for parents

The background details will usually contain information on previous assessments, the current and previous schools and some reasons for the assessment. This is normally at the beginning of a report and would usually only provide a brief outline. This is important as it would indicate who initiated the referral for the assessment, if there were any concerns relating to the child's progress and, if so, the type of concerns.

2. Test behaviour/attention and concentration

Christopher attended very well throughout a fairly lengthy assessment. He showed interest in most of the test materials, particularly those items where there was some 'hands on' activity. He was aware that he required quite a bit of time to complete some of the activities and would frequently ask if he was taking too long. Nevertheless, he appeared quite confident and was willing to engage in conversation and responded well to questions put to him regarding the test and his current performances in class.

Explanatory comments for parents

This section of the report can provide some indication of the child's interest level as well as attention and concentration. It must be remembered that a test is quite a formal procedure, and although it is important to reassure the child in some way, assessors cannot give any direct positive or negative feedback.

Although it can be difficult for some children to sit and undertake a test that may last well over one hour, this experience will provide some indication of the child's potential for attending and concentrating. Many children, however, usually respond well to the individual attention shown by the tester. If the child has significant concentration difficulties, it is possible for assessors to administer the assessment in sections.

3. Test used

Some of the tests that can be used in an assessment are listed below, together with explanations of the purpose of these tests. Some psychologists have preferences for one test over another and some tests may be more widely used in certain countries.

Ability tests

Wechsler Intelligence Scale for Children

This (Figure 2.2) is essentially an IQ test that provides a verbal IQ score, a non-verbal score and a full-scale IQ. It also provides a profile – this can be called a cognitive profile as it relates to areas of information processing, and the word 'cognitive' means thinking and processing. It is possible, therefore, to observe the different areas of strengths and weaknesses at a glance.

There are many other cognitive-type tests that can be used such as Raven's Progressive Matrices and the British Assessment Scales. In the USA, comprehensive tests such as the Woodcock–Johnson, the Wechsler Individual Achievement Tests of Basic Reading, Spelling and Numerical Operations and the Monroe Sherman Tests of Reading, Writing and Motor Speed are also used. The tests that can be used are too numerous to list here, except to note that, generally speaking, tests tend to be cognitive (measuring ability), attainment (measuring performances) or skill specific (measuring factors such as laterality, balance or visual acuity).

Irrespective of the test(s) that are used, it is important to obtain a description of the test, as in Figure 2.2, and to obtain some reasons why this particular test was used.

Attainment tests

Attainment tests refers to tests that focus levels of performances in attainments such as reading, spelling, writing and number work. There are many different types of such tests and parents would normally receive some information on the type of tests that are used and what they aim to find out. An example of one such attainment test is shown below.

Wechsler Objective Reading Dimensions

This consists of three tests: word reading, spelling and reading comprehension. It provides an age-related percentile score for these items, which is a score out of 100 to represent the position in the general

Verbal scale

Information	This tests general knowledge and can be considered a test of long-term memory
Similarities	Understanding of verbal concepts and the connections between ideas and objects
Arithmetic	Mental operations – this involves short-term auditory memory, holding information in head for short time and repeating it back to the tester
Vocabulary	Verbal expression – the ability to express oneself verbally through an explanation of the meaning of words. The words are graded in difficulty
Comprehension	Verbal understanding – this involves an explanation of some common facts and situations. The child may have to give an elaborated response to the question to get full marks
Digit-span	Short-term auditory memory – this involves holding numbers provided by the tester and repeating them

Performance scale

Picture completion	Visual perception, i.e. the ability to observe visual information and identify a missing feature
Coding	Psycho-motor speed – visual memory, pencil and paper that involves copying and remembering symbols. This is a timed test and involves processing speed
Picture arrangement	Visual sequencing, the ability to arrange pictures in a logical sequence that can describe the sequence of an event
Block design	Visuo-spatial awareness.
Object assembly	Visual organisation, speed of processing

Figure 2.2 Wechsler Intelligence Scale for Children (WISC) – summary of sub-tests

age-related population. For example, a score of 50 percentile for reading would indicate that a child is exactly average for his or her chronological age for reading.

There are other attainment tests that also focus on the above, as well as other areas such as reading fluency and the competence the child shows in phonological awareness and phonological processing. These latter factors relate to the child's knowledge of sounds and awareness of sounds in words. This can be a core difficulty experienced by children with dyslexia and is therefore an important aspect of an assessment. It is also possible for phonological awareness to be assessed informally by the teacher and this type of information can be available to supplement a formal assessment.

4. Results and interpretation of results

The example below is taken from an assessment report and the actual report is in *italics*. Comments and explanations for parents are found below each section of the italicised report.

Comment on results of cognitive test
The results in Figure 2.3 reveal a cognitive profile for a dyslexic child. Not every dyslexic profile is the same, and not every one will look like the one in Figure 2.3. It is important for parents to recognise that many different aspects contribute to an assessment and diagnosis, and although the cognitive profile is important, it is not sufficient on its own. Additionally, because cognitive profiles can differ for dyslexic children

Wechsler Intelligence Scale for Children (WISC III)			
Verbal scale		*Performance scale*	
Information	14	Picture completion	15
Similarities	11	Coding	7
Arithmetic	9	Picture arrangement	16
Vocabulary	12	Block design	14
Comprehension	9	Object assembly	13
Digit-span	(6)		
Verbal IQ	105	Performance IQ	121
	Full-scale IQ	114	
Range = 20			
Average = 10			

Figure 2.3 Results: example from cognitive test

each one requires explanation and interpretation. This is normally explained in the report. An example of this is shown below.

Cognitive assessment

In the Wechsler Intelligence Scale, Christopher scored in the high average range overall. Christopher scored above average in both the verbal and the performance (non-verbal) scales, although in the non-verbal scale he did score in the high range. This indicates that Christopher has abilities in both these areas, but has significant abilities in the visual area.

There is, however, evidence of some discrepancies within both these scales – the verbal and the performance scales.

Explanatory comment for parents

It is sometimes useful to compare the overall scores in the verbal scale with those in the performance (non-verbal) scales. Quite often, but not always, children with dyslexia can show a significantly higher score in the non-verbal scales than in the verbal. This is because the verbal scales deal with language skills and remembering and using information with no assistance or cues from the tester. This can be challenging for children with dyslexia as language is often their weaker area; also, because no cues are provided, it can be difficult for them to access some words and information.

The performance scales tend to focus on the visual area, and this can be one of the strengths shown by children with dyslexia.

However, as indicated earlier, one of the most revealing aspects about an assessment is the pattern of scores and, in particular, any discrepancies between scores in the same area. It can be noted in the sample report in Figure 2.3 that this type of discrepancy may be evident. It can be seen in Figure 2.3 that the verbal scale scores range from 6 in digit-span to 14 in information. As this represents a wide range of scores, this pattern can be referred to as a discrepancy. For a verbal IQ of 105 it would be expected that a child would have an approximately average score in digit-span. Some explanation therefore needs to be sought as to why the digit-span score is discrepant with the other scores. Any discrepancies noted within the verbal and performance scales would be worthy of comment in the report.

Verbal scales

In the verbal scale, Christopher scored in the high range in general knowledge and above average in vocabulary and in his understanding of verbal concepts. In comprehension Christopher scored slightly lower, in the low average range. This sub-test requires an elaborated response and Christopher found this quite challenging. He would have benefited from some cues to help to provide an extended response, but this is not permitted in the test situation.

In the digit-span and arithmetic sub-tests, Christopher scored around/below average. Both these sub-tests relate to short-term and working memory and these can be challenging for many young children with a dyslexic processing style. It was noted throughout the assessment that Christopher did require the maximum time for some of the tasks, and if time limits were to be imposed on classroom tasks he may not perform to his optimum ability.

Explanatory comment for parents

It is sometimes unusual for children with dyslexia to score as high as this in the information sub-test. A high score in this sub-test does, to an extent, rely on obtaining information from reading and remembering that information, which can be difficult for children with dyslexia. However, information can now be obtained from video/DVD and from computer sources such as games and the internet. But, generally, children with dyslexia can have a difficulty with this sub-test as it does require recalling the information immediately and without any assistance. In the report shown in Figure 2.3 it can be noted that the child scored slightly above average in vocabulary. Sometimes the performance of a child with dyslexia can be deceptive in this sub-test. The parents may believe that the child has an excellent vocabulary, as he or she may well have, but the requirements of this sub-test demands that the child provides an elaborated response to the meaning of a word. This can be quite difficult for a dyslexic child as it involves verbal expression in an organised manner as well as verbal elaboration. It can be noted in the above assessment that the score in the sub-test – similarities (this relates to verbal concepts) – is also around average. Again this requires language skills and working out a problem with no assistance. This sub-test may ask: 'In what way are two items similar – for example, a blueberry and blue sky?' (Note that this is not an actual item from the test.) What one is looking for in this sub-test is how these items can be grouped into categories, e.g. in this case colour. It can occasionally take children with dyslexia a little time to actually understand what is required in this type of task and they may not score as highly as would be suggested by their abilities and performances in class work.

Similarly in the comprehension sub-test in Figure 2.3, the score is around average, but again this was because the child did not elaborate sufficiently in some of the responses. This is fairly common with dyslexic children.

The remaining two sub-tests in the verbal scale are arithmetic and digit-span. Both of these can be very challenging for dyslexic children as they require working and short-term memory skills. This means that information has to be held in the child's mind for a short time while he or she undertakes some processing activity. This activity can include, for example, reciting numbers backwards or working out a mental arithmetic problem. Many children with dyslexia would have difficulty with this and therefore their scores in these sub-tests can be much lower than in some of the other verbal sub-tests.

Performance scales

In the performance (non-verbal) area a different pattern can be noted and Christopher's scores were generally higher compared to those in the verbal scales. Christopher scored in the above average range in all the sub-tests in the visual area, except for coding. This includes those sub-tests relating to visual sequencing, visual/spatial ability, visual perception and visual organisation. In the coding sub-test, which is a test of visuo-motor speed, Christopher scored well above average. This was not surprising since he required almost the maximum time in many of the sub-tests. Speed of processing is an important element in class work and in examinations, and in view of his performances in the timed tests in this assessment Christopher will require extra time in examinations.

Explanatory comment for parents
The performance scales relate more to visual skills than to verbal skills and children with dyslexia score often much higher in these sub-tests.

In Figure 2.3 the child scored high in the visual sub-tests, but well below average in the coding sub-test. The coding sub-test relates to processing speed when copying symbols and it is very common for children with dyslexia to have difficulty with this task. It was also noted in Figure 2.3 that the child required maximum time in some of the visual sub-tests. There are time penalties in some of the items in the performance sub-test. Children with dyslexia may well complete the task correctly, but because they take more time to complete the task their scores in the sub-tests are adversely affected. This has implications for additional time being allocated for examinations and for class work.

Summary of cognitive assessment

In general, therefore, the cognitive assessment shows that Christopher has high average abilities in both the verbal and visual areas. He had a tendency to score higher in this assessment in visual activities, but would have scored even higher, had it not been for the timed factor in most of the performance sub-tests. In the verbal scales he did find some of the sub-tests quite challenging, particularly those relating to short-term memory. This profile has many characteristics of dyslexia.

Explanatory comment for parents

This part of the report should provide a short and clear summary of the cognitive assessment and indicate the child's relative strengths and weaknesses. Some preliminary diagnosis can also be offered at this stage.

There will be a section in the report on the results of attainments. This refers to the child's level of reading, spelling and writing, and perhaps listening and reading comprehension.

Attainments

Test used: Wechsler Objective Reading Dimensions (WORD)
Reading age: 9 years
Spelling age: 8 years 6 months

In the attainment tests Christopher scored well below his age level in reading accuracy and in spelling. He also has some difficulty with reading fluency and often had to re-read text. Christopher scored well below his age level. He had difficulty in decoding unknown and multi-syllabic words and in spelling regular and irregular words. He showed both phonological and visual errors in his reading and spelling. His handwriting style was also inconsistent.

Explanatory comment for parents

Reading fluency is important as this helps with the comprehension of text. If the child's reading rate is slow, he or she may well lose the meaning of the passage and will inevitably have to re-read it. Re-reading is quite common for children with dyslexia but it does require more time and effort. It can be of concern if the child is performing well below his or her chronological age. Certainly two years of a lag in a primary age child would be cause for concern. Sometimes the discrepancy that is used by some education authorities relates more to the difference between (a) the projected level of attainments based on the IQ score and (b) the actual level. Identification based on this, and other types of discrepancy criteria, is still a matter of controversy and debate among professionals. This is because the level of discrepancy that can access support is usually set at a certain level, which means that children who may be in need of additional support can be neglected because they do not fall within the specific discrepancy range set by the education authority.

In relation to the pattern of errors in reading and spelling, phonological-type errors can often be noted in children with dyslexia. As an example of this, 'bark' may be written as 'barck' and 'show' written as 'sow'. It is, however, not uncommon for some children with dyslexia to also show visual errors and they may add extra letters or omit some letters. As was noted in the report, it is also worth referring to the child's writing style. Many children with dyslexia have an inconsistent style with the slope of letters and the use of capitals and small letters being inconsistently applied.

Most reports will indicate the educational implications of the results of the assessment. There are different ways of doing this: some can be general while others can be very specific and may refer to the curriculum or the practice in that area or country. Any general implications may be followed up with specific recommendations.

5. Educational implications

Christopher has dyslexia and this can be noted particularly in relation to his processing speed, short-term memory and his reading and spelling pattern. This clearly will have some effect on his classroom performances and he will require special arrangements such as extra time for examinations. He will also require specific structured and multisensory programmes to help with reading and spelling. He may also benefit from some form of additional support in the classroom and opportunities for working in group activities.

Explanatory comment for parents
Clearly a diagnosis, if appropriate, will be useful as often the label has to be applied before certain levels of support can be offered. The implications of the above is that some specific programmes can be useful. There are many different types of programmes and some can be used successfully at home. It is best, however, to link with the teachers on this aspect and obtain advice from the school or from a dyslexia association.

Some general principles can apply to programmes for children with dyslexia. This aspect will be developed in the next chapter of this book but, generally, such programmes should be multi-sensory – that means that they should allow for visual, auditory, kinaesthetic and tactile input. 'Visual' means that the child should be able to learn from the programme from visual stimuli, such as pictures; 'auditory' means that the sounds of words should be made clear in the programme; and 'kinaesthetic' means that there should be some activities based on the programme where the child has to act out, or benefit from experiential learning through using the programme. This can be tracing the shape of a letter, or being involved in a dramatic production based on text. 'Tactile' refers to being able to touch, for example, the words or the letters. This can be done through using wooden letters. Computer programs can be both kinaesthetic and tactile.

The issue of additional support for their child can be a confusing issue for parents. It is a common assumption that one-to-one teaching can benefit learners with dyslexia and, indeed, in some circumstances this is the case. But the important point is that this does *not* necessarily *need* to be the case. Learners with dyslexia can often make better and perhaps more appropriate progress with in-class support or working in small groups. Much depends on the nature of the programs being offered.

Most reports will contain some form of specific recommendations. These may detail actual programs or give some general indications of the type of program that would be beneficial. This can be seen in the following recommendations from the report given in Figure 2.3.

6. Recommendations

Reading fluency

It is important that Christopher develops fluency in reading as this can also help with comprehension. This can be achieved through practice in reading and engaging in activities such as paired reading. Reading for meaning helps to develop fluency, so it is important that Christopher has a clear picture of the background to the story and an overview of the text before reading it. This will help him to become familiar with the concepts, ideas and vocabulary of the text. Pre-reading discussion is therefore very useful.

There are many sources of high interest and low vocabulary readers in both the UK and the USA, as well as in Australia, New Zealand and Canada. In the UK the Hi–Lo readers from LDA, Cambridge and from Barrington Stoke Ltd (www.barringtonstoke.co.uk) can be beneficial in relation to reading fluency.

The BBC Education (Scotland) Series of history books for primary aged children written by Richard Dargie provide an excellent and stim-ulating read for young children. The books, which are on popular topics such as the Vikings and the Romans, include colourful illustrations and are written in clear text with added features such as date time lines and glossaries. The above is just an example, but many children's books have been written and produced in this manner and parents should look at how the book is produced and presented and the level of vocabulary it contains, as well as its interest rating.

Class/teacher discussion

Christopher will benefit from discussion during and following any task he is engaged in. This will help to provide him with practice at thinking about problems and resolving any comprehension difficulties he may experience in the text, or in related activities. This will help to extend his comprehension and provide opportunities for verbal expression.

Speed of processing

There are a number of computer programs and game activities that can help with this, as many of these help to develop reaction skills and encourage the child to process more quickly. Nevertheless, extra time in course work and in examinations is essential.

'Inspiration'/or other similar programs

The software programs called 'Kidspiration' up to age 8 and 'Inspiration' (age 8 to adult) are very useful and can help with creative writing. There are other similar programs available that can help with the organisation of information in preparation for essay writing. 'Inspiration' enables the user to create a visual map of ideas similar to mind mapping. The software includes its own library of shapes, symbols and pictures that can be utilised within a variety of colour schemes.

Study skills

- *Study skills programs would also be helpful, focusing on the identification of key points and developing schema and concepts. These aspects would help Christopher to develop reading speed skills and ensure that the development of comprehension skills are not neglected.*
- *Essentially study skills involves focusing on each of the stages of the information-processing cycle – input, cognition and output. Some suggestions for each of these stages are shown below:*

Input

- *Acknowledge the students preferred learning style*
- *Present information in small units*
- *Use over-learning and this involves the use of a range of materials*
- *Present key points, particularly at the initial stage of learning new material.*

Cognition

- *Encourage organisational strategies. This means that the new material to be learned should be organised into meaningful chunks or categories at each of the information-processing stages.*
- *Relate information to previous knowledge to ensure that concepts are clear and the information can be placed into a learning framework, or schema, by the learner.*
- *Use specific memory strategies such as Mind Mapping©, Memory Booster© (Lucid Research Ltd) and mnemonics.*

Output

- *Use headings and sub-headings in written work to help to provide a structure.*
- *Encourage the use of summaries in order to identify the key points.*

Computer programs

There are many very useful computer programs available in every country. Such programs as Word Shark and Word Shark 3 can be useful as the Word Shark program includes use of phonics, onset and rime, homophones, spelling rules, common letter patterns, visual and auditory patterns, prefixes, suffixes and alphabet and dictionary skills. Word Shark 3 is suitable for ages 5–14 and also offers 36 different games that use sound, graphics and text to teach and reinforce word recognition and spelling. Other suitable programs include Starspell, which teaches word level literacy skills using the look-say-cover-write-check approach. Another game-type computer program that can also be useful is Nessy. This is suitable from age 5 onwards and is a complete literacy program for reading, spelling and writing skills.

*The computer program mentioned earlier – Memory Booster©
(www.memory-booster.com) from Lucid Research Ltd (www.lucid-research.com) – is a stimulating and fun way to improve children's
memory skills. The program encourages independent learning and is
presented in the form of an adventure game set in Pooter's Castle.
Pooter, the master computer, has lost his memory and needs help from
the child to recover it. There are built-in cartoon rewards that use hu-
morous and motivating graphics that help the child to stay on task.
Memory Booster© therefore aims to develop verbal and visual memory
skills, is suitable for use at home as well as at school, and is targeted
at children in the 4–11+ age group.*

Keyboard skills

*It is always useful for young children to develop keyboard skills and
there are some computer programs such as KAZ (Keyboarding A–Z)
that can help children to acquire competence in using the keyboard.*

Resources

*This section would normally contain a list of resources and websites
that can be accessed and are useful for parents and teachers. This list
has been omitted from this sample report as Chapter 3 and Chapter 9
will deal with this aspect more fully.*

*It is important, however, that the resources section contains more
than a list of books and programs. Some form of annotation would
be helpful for parents to enable them to see at a glance which of the
resources would be suitable for them and which are aimed at teachers.
Some reports may actually detail specific resources aimed at parents
and there are an increasing number of very useful websites. (A list of
relevant websites can be found in the links page in Gavin Reid's home
page – www.gavinreid.co.uk – and in Chapter 9.)*

Explanatory comment for parents
As indicated above, it is important that as a parent you obtain some
guidance in the report, or in the follow-up meeting. Information on the

resources that can be readily and usefully accessed by parents will be particularly useful.

7. Conclusion

In summary, Christopher is of high average ability overall in the test situation, although in the visual area he has significant abilities. Christopher is dyslexic. Some of his scores in this assessment may be lower due to the nature of the test situation. This is particularly the case with the comprehension score – no help can be provided in a test situation such as this one – and it was noted that with prompts and cues Christopher may have been able to elaborate on some of his responses. This has implications for teaching and underlines the value of small group teaching and small group discussion.

Christopher did show many above-average scores in both the performance (non-verbal) scales and in the verbal scales. This is very encouraging as these abilities can be used to help to develop reading fluency, memory and other processing skills.

Explanatory comment for parents

What you are looking for here is a straightforward summing up of the assessment. This means that you will be able to read the conclusion and obtain a fairly accurate picture of the assessment and the implications.

Assessment issues

An American, Glen Young, suggests that, according to an old joke in the USA, the best way to 'cure' a learning disability is to cross a State line. The standards in different States for diagnosis can vary greatly from 1 to 3 standard deviations. This means that the percentage of children who are recognised by the State as having learning disabilities will differ from State to State. He gives the example of 7.2% (Rhode Island, Massachusetts) to 2.5% (Georgia, Kentucky) (Young, 2003, personal communication). Examples such as these can be noted in most countries, which can be confusing for parents and, of course, for the child.

There are a number of issues related to this, and to assessment and identification of dyslexia generally, that can be of concern to parents. These include consistency, availability and the use of labels and terminology.

Consistency

One of the main issues in relation to assessment is the need for consistency so that parents will not be confused by the kind of situation described above. This, however, is easier said than done as education authorities may have their own set of criteria and procedures for identifying disabilities. It is nevertheless important that parents should not incur additional stress when moving to another area of the country. Written reports from the previous school can be a good safeguard and these can at least let the new school know something about the child.

Availability

There is a concern about the availability of an assessment. Schools can differ in the availability of psychologists and the availability of teachers trained in dyslexia who can carry out an assessment. As indicated above, however, teachers can accumulate considerable knowledge of the child from observation in the classroom and discussions with parents. Many teachers now have an awareness of dyslexia and can seek to find out more from colleagues, books and the websites on dyslexia.

Despite the increased knowledge of dyslexia and the enhanced awareness on dyslexia within the teaching profession, there are still identification issues in many countries. Some of these are resolved through discussions between school and parents, others are resolved through political means by parents making representations and exerting pressure on government representatives, and the final resort for many is litigation. This is far from ideal, is confrontational and can be expensive and destructive of relations between home and school. Often litigation arises because of the different perspectives held by schools, parents and parent associations on dyslexia. But sometimes, when confronted by a school or an education system that claims not to recognise the specific needs of children with dyslexia, parents, often in despair, have to resort to the courts. In the UK the Tribunal system and the appeals procedure have resulted in many decisions going in favour of parents. In some other countries, such as the USA, a considerable number of successful court actions have been made by parent representatives on behalf of the child. Usually one successful action can be all that it takes to ensure that children with dyslexia are identified.

Use of labels and terminology

In some areas, and in some countries, there can still be a reluctance to use the label dyslexia. Sometimes other labels are used, such as specific reading difficulty or, in some cases, no label at all is used. At the same time it needs to be recognised that a label in itself will not provide an answer to dyslexia and schools who do not use a label may well be providing appropriate input. It is worth considering, however, that young people with dyslexia need to understand what dyslexia is as this will help them deal with it more effectively as they go through school and into adult life. A label, if appropriate, therefore may be useful as the first step in this process.

Summary

This chapter has provided some guidance for parents in relation to the assessment process as well as information on the details and content of an assessment. This involves looking at the roles and responsibilities of different professional groups such as class teachers, specialist teacher and other professionals as well as the actual role that parents play in an assessment.

This chapter also provides some guidance for parents in interpreting specialised reports. Sometimes such reports can be cloaked in jargon and technical terms that may be confusing for parents. It is therefore important that the results of an assessment are fully explained to parents and, if appropriate, to the child. Even if a formal assessment does not take place, teachers will have information on the child through class assessment and ongoing monitoring. This type of information is also extremely important and needs to be shared with parents.

The chapter has attempted to provide as full an explanation as possible of the type of comments and recommendations that can be found in assessment reports. Parents are very often keen to do something at home that can help their child. The sample report in this chapter indicates the type of activities that can benefit their child and how they may participate in such activities. This point will be followed up in the next chapter.

Chapter 3

How dyslexic children learn and how parents can help

There is a great deal of evidence to suggest that dyslexic difficulties are associated with factors related to the learning process. These factors, known as 'cognitive' factors, are often referred to in psychologists' reports and have been mentioned in the previous two chapters of this book. 'Cognition' refers to how information is processed – that is, how children understand, remember and use that information when learning new material and when recalling previously learned material. This chapter will examine these cognitive aspects of learning and aims to help parents to understand how children with dyslexia learn. It also suggests how parents may be able to help and complement what is being done in school.

Information processing

When we learn anything – no matter what we are learning – the brain engages in a number of processes. These processes are important for effective learning and are particularly important for children with dyslexia. The research suggests that dyslexic children may not process information efficiently.

There are many strategies that can be used to make the process of learning more effective and parents, as well as teachers, can play a part in this. It is important to consider the different stages of learning in this process, which are:

1. The input stage, which occurs when the learner takes in the information.
2. The cognitive stage, when the information has to be processed – that is, understood and organised to enable the learner to access it for future use. To do this the learner has to fully understand the information so that it can be organised and 'filed' appropriately as this will make recall more efficient.
3. The output stage, when the learner displays his or her knowledge and understanding of the information that has been learned. This can be in written form or, perhaps, in some other manner such as through drama or by discussion. This learning, or information-processing, cycle is discussed in more detail below.

Input

Information processing begins when we either see, or hear, what we want to learn. Often, of course, we have to do both at the same time, and this is called the input stage. In this stage we take in information and try to make sense of it so that it can be understood and remembered. If we have difficulty in recalling information at a later date it may be because the information was not effectively processed in the first place. I am sure we have all experienced listening to someone and then asking that person to repeat it: 'Sorry, I was not really listening, something else distracted me.' In order to process something effectively it is crucial that the information is taken in and understood at the initial stage of learning. This is important irrespective of whether the task is learning a new word or studying a picture. We need to go through the same processes.

The input stage is particularly important for children with dyslexia because they may have a weakness in absorbing information, particularly if it is presented in a certain way. Although the most common means of absorbing information is through the visual and auditory modalities – that is, seeing and hearing – information can also be understood through the kinaesthetic and tactile modalities. 'Kinaesthetic' means experiencing, and by participating in a drama, play or undertaking 'field' work where learning is experiential, the child is using the kinaesthetic modality. 'Tactile' refers to being able to touch an object and this 'hands on' learning can be very suitable for some children. For example, by working with and touching wooden alphabet letters, the dyslexic child is using his or her tactile modality and this can help to reinforce the shape of the letters.

The auditory modality is usually the weakest one for children with dyslexia, while the visual, kinaesthetic and tactile modalities are usually stronger. It is therefore better to present information in a multi-sensory manner that uses all the modalities.

Cognition

This is the part of learning that refers to how we understand and remember information: how we make sense of information, how we relate it to what we already know, and how we can categorise new information and store it away for recall at a later date. Much of this is done without thinking too much, *except* when we come across a difficult piece of information that challenges us. Then we have to make an effort to:

- understand the information
- decide what it means
- consider what it refers to
- think of what it is similar to, and
- determine how we might remember it in the future.

This process may take much time and effort, but this is the process the dyslexic child has to go through when he or she is learning most language-based items. For children with dyslexia almost all language-based learning can be a challenge.

The key aspects of cognition are:

- Comprehension
- Memory
- Organisation.

It is important that information is understood at the time of learning as this will enable recall. Once the information is understood, some strategies can be used to help to remember it. First, however, it must be understood, and parents have a role to play in this by reinforcing the learning that takes place in school.

Output

Output refers to how children can display what they know. In our education system, which is highly dominated by examinations, the output is very often the written modality. This, however, can be the weakest modality for children with dyslexia. For that reason they require additional support to prepare for examinations and to help them to organise and develop writing skills. Since much of this depends on organisational skills, parents can help by asking questions and helping the children to organise items into different groups or categories. This will be developed further in this chapter.

Comprehension

Comprehension refers to understanding, which is an essential aspect of learning. While it is possible to learn through sheer rote learning and memorising information, this is not really desirable. If information is learned without any real understanding, it will not be retained as effectively as it would be if the information was fully understood. Furthermore, if there is understanding, the child will be able to use the information in a range of different ways. Understanding is therefore vital for effective learning. This is an important point in relation to dyslexia. Comprehension can often be neglected as teaching may be more focused on the actual skill involved in reading and spelling. This may unintentionally relegate language experience and comprehension to a less important role.

Children with dyslexia may have a long-standing difficulty with reading fluency and reading accuracy, and for that reason it is important that they develop language comprehension as they may have to rely very heavily on 'context' – i.e. what the text is about and the background to the text – in order to gain meaning from the text. This can be done through language experience and quite often the text can be comprehended from only a few cues. In most texts there are many words that can be challenging for a child with dyslexia. In order to teach the child any text it is best to focus on the key words. Sometimes there may be only a few key words, but these will be sufficient to provide him or her with some context and meaning for the events in the text.

Pre-reading discussion

It is important to engage in pre-reading discussion with the child before he or she reads the text. This means that if your son or daughter is about to make a start on homework that involves reading, you should both discuss the background to the text before the homework is attempted. There is a body of research that suggests that pre-reading discussion is one of the best predictors of a successful outcome in a reading activity.

Some questions that can provide a framework for pre-reading discussion are shown below. It can be more effective if the parent reads the passage first to the child, or perhaps uses paired reading (see later in this chapter), and then suggests some questions that the child should think about as the passage is being read.

A possible framework for pre-reading questions

- Who are the main characters?
- How do you know they are the main characters?
- What do you know about the characters?
- What are they doing?
- Where is the passage (book) set?
- Can you describe the scene?
- What happens in the story?
- How does it end?
- Do you think it was a good ending? Why or why not?

This will not only provide the child with a sequence for the narrative and the key characters in the story, but it will also help him or her to form opinions on the text. It is through forming opinions that a higher level of comprehension will develop.

This type of activity should be engaged in whether the child is or is not a competent reader. The child may be lagging in decoding (skills in reading accuracy), but it is important that he or she does not lose ground in language comprehension, as children with dyslexia will usually have good comprehension skills.

If the child is about to tackle a book, it may also be an idea to obtain a video of the book beforehand. This will help to provide a visual image of the scene and an overall context for the main characters and the events. Certainly this type of activity to enhance language comprehension will take place in school, but parents need to be aware of this to reinforce it at home.

Memory skills

Children with dyslexia will usually have difficulties in remembering, retaining and recalling information. This may be due to short-term or working memory difficulties, but it may also be due to a naming difficulty – i.e. difficulty in recalling the name of an object or place. It is important, therefore, to encourage the use of strategies that may facilitate remembering and recall. Such strategies can include:

- Repetition and over-learning
- Mnemonics
- Mind Mapping©
- Other visual strategies that the learner may develop.

Short-term memory

Short-term memory refers to holding a piece of information in your head for a very brief period of time, which could be as short as half a second. However, this period of time is sufficient to enable the learner to process the information. Some learners, however, have difficulty in retaining information for even a brief period and the information is often lost to them.

I am sure everyone has been in the position where they have lost information before it could be processed. A good example of this is when the film credits roll up the screen at the end of a film. It is unlikely that you have the processing capabilities to remember, or even read, them all as they so often appear and disappear before you have had a chance to read them. This is because your short-term memory is not equipped to deal with so much information in such a short space of time.

Repetition and over-learning

Children with dyslexia often have short-term memory difficulties. This can make learning any new material very time-consuming as information has often to be over-learned before it can be retained. Repetition and rehearsal of materials can take a great deal of time. Information will eventually be learned in this way but it is important that over-learning should be carried out using a range of learning experiences. Parents can have a role to play in this and can follow up school learning using different opportunities for learning, such as shopping and going on family excursions.

Rote learning and repetition of information can have drawbacks. The material learned can be at a superficial level and it may not be accompanied by a deeper understanding. Before deep processing can occur the information has to be understood and used meaningfully in different ways, and rote learning does not really allow for this.

In order to maximise the effect of over-learning, it is important that a multi-sensory method of learning is used. Retention of the material to be learned can be accomplished through oral, visual, auditory and kinaesthetic modes. The learner should be able to see, hear, say and touch the materials to be learned. This reinforces the input stimuli and helps to consolidate the information for use, meaning and transfer to other areas. There are implications here for school as well as for parents; for example, the use of movement, perhaps drama, to enhance the kinaesthetic mode of learning can be beneficial and, of course, this type of activity can be done after school. Many parents have reported how beneficial after-school activities such as swimming clubs and music activities can be. These can certainly help to boost self-esteem, but organised activities after school can also help to develop over-learning as the child has to use listening skills and develop interaction skills with others.

Mnemonics

Mnemonics is the use of characters, numbers or symbols that can help people to remember items. Try to think of how you remember the shopping you need when at a supermarket. Some people make a list; others, however, make symbols for different kinds of items such as kitchen items, bathroom items and food. Mnemonics can be auditory or visual, or both auditory and visual, and can involve numbers or figures. Auditory mnemonics may take the form of rhyming or alliteration while visual mnemonics can be used by relating the material to be remembered to a familiar scene, such as the classroom or, in the example above, the supermarket.

Mind Mapping©

Mind mapping is a technique that is now widely used (Buzan, 1993). It can be a simple or a sophisticated strategy depending on how it is developed. It is used to help the learner to remember a considerable amount of information and encourages children to think of, and develop, the main ideas of the material to be learned.

Mind maps are very individual and someone else's mind map may not be meaningful to every learner. It is important, therefore, that children create their own mind maps, in order to help both with understanding the key concepts and in the retention and recall of facts. Mind maps can therefore be a learning tool as well as a tool for the retention of information. A mind map can help the child to remember information, but it also helps the child to organise information and this, in turn, can help with understanding.

Elaborate versions of mind maps can be constructed using pictorial images, symbols and different colours.

Organisation

One of the most frequently displayed characteristics of dyslexia is that relating to organisation. Organisational difficulties can be seen as a right-brain trait and can be accompanied by spontaneity and perhaps creativity. Although these factors in some situations can be advantageous, there are many occasions where lack of organisational skills can be disabling. Although it is not desirable to attempt to change the processing style of a dyslexic person, some support and guidance may be necessary to help with organisation.

For the dyslexic child, organisational difficulties can result in problems with homework, planning essays, adhering to a time-table and remembering information. It is important, therefore, to help the dyslexic person to develop a more efficient organisational system.

Organisational system

Factors that can help with organisation are:

- Time-tabling
- Routine
- Filing
- Buddies
- Presentation.

Some suggestions for this are shown below:

Time-tabling

- Colour-coding
- Adhering to routine
- Planning in advance
- Visible time-table.

The above points can be developed to make time-tabling more efficient and more easily remembered. The use of colours can help. For example, physical education may take place every Tuesday afternoon – in the time-table this can be colour-coded, perhaps red with a star because the child has to remember to bring equipment. It is best for the child to develop his or her own system but it is important that some system is attempted, especially when items have to be brought to school and homework has to be remembered.

Routine

A routine can be helpful as it can reinforce organisation skills over a period of time.

Similarly, planning in advance can be very useful as advanced planning actually helps with organisation – the problem is remembering where the child put the plan! It may be useful for the child to have a separate book for writing plans. For example, how to get to places, rooms in the school, venues for after-school clubs, plans for revision and plans for leisure.

Filing

It is important that the child with dyslexia realises the importance of filing. Again colour-coding can be used and there are all sorts of decorative and unusual filing systems, coloured boxes, portable filing cases, filing drawers and all sorts of box files that it is possible to encourage and motivate the child to make some effort with filing. Sometimes, when they have to, people with dyslexia can have quite an intricate and sophisticated filing system that works for them! This is important as it must be from their own conception because they will then be happier to use it more fully.

Buddies

The use of buddies can also be helpful. This is when two people can help each other by reminding each other of events, and they agree in advance what each has to remind the other about. Sometimes when you have to do something for someone else it is easier to recall and remember it.

Presentation

Children with dyslexia often need help to organise presentations. This can apply to presentations they have to make orally in class or in written work. It is important that they are encouraged to plan presentations and form some type of structure to help with this. An example of how to organise reports and presentations is shown below:

- What materials do I need?
- How am I going to start?

- What are the main points?
- How am I going to put this across?
- Do I need assistance from anyone?
- What message do I want the audience to receive?
- What is my conclusion?

Whether it is a presentation being carried out by an 8-year-old dyslexic boy or an 18-year-old at university, it is important to develop some kind of plan. In fact, this is just as important for the younger child as it is for the older student because it is important to practise organising presentations of written work, and the earlier practice in this type of planning takes place, the better.

Reading

How do children learn to read and why is it so difficult for children with dyslexia? There are two basic models of reading. One is called the bottom-up and the other top-down.

The *bottom-up* model refers to the need to learn the individual sub-skills of reading before tackling the meaning and understanding of text. This would mean that only text that is within the child's reading age should be given.

In relation to the bottom-up model of reading there are many different methods and strategies of teaching these sub-skills. For example, some children may rely on a visual route to learning to read but will still need to remember the individual letters and the groups of letters that make specific sounds such as 'ough', which is a common word ending.

Usually when the bottom-up method is taught the teacher would start with each of the letters of the alphabet so that the child knew not only the main letters but also the sequence of letters in the alphabet. Once those have been taught the child would then learn different letter combinations that make up words. The teacher would also show examples of these combinations of letters as they appear in words.

The *top-down* model, on the other hand, would focus on the use of the words in language and the teacher would highlight the importance of meaning in text. This would imply that a child does not have to read every word but can rely to a great extent on context and language experience. Using this model, background knowledge is important as the child has to make inferences about what might happen and the words that would very likely appear. The child can obtain this from discussion and from taped books or videos.

The implications of these models for parents

Although the teaching of reading is the responsibility of the school, there are implications for parents. It is important that parents are aware of how the school is teaching reading and the programmes that are being used by the teacher. Different reading programmes will have a different emphasis. For example, you may have two programmes that are both bottom-up but each will be structured in a different way and can have a different emphasis. This highlights the importance of liaising with the school to enable you to obtain advice on the best way to reinforce the teaching of reading at home.

Consistency with school

As indicated above, it is important that the parents know how reading is taught in school. There are a number of activities that parents can do at home that can help to develop the reading skills of their dyslexic child. It can, however, be more productive if parents use this time with their child to reinforce the reading activities that are taking place in school. For example, if the child is being taught specific sounds or spelling rules, then these can be followed up at home by parents. Generally speaking, however, any kind of literacy activity will be useful for the child, but it is essential to ensure that the child does not become 'switched off' from reading because of the demands it places on him or her. The role of the parents, therefore, is to help to instil an interest in reading, perhaps through discussion, or reading to the child, or reading together. These can minimise the demands of the reading task for the dyslexic child.

Reading practice

Practice in reading is important. The reading material does not need to be established works of literature, but in fact can be anything that is going to interest the child. Newspapers and magazines can be just as useful as sources of reading material, and perhaps more motivating than some books. The main point is that practice is essential, and it is through practice that reading can become part of the child's routine. It is important to try to establish this. The Hi–Lo readers, which are characterised by the high-interest and low-vocabulary level of the book, can be ideal for children with dyslexia.

Games

Games can be an excellent way of reinforcing reading. Although there are a number of commercially produced games (see Chapter 9), parents can use game-type activities, even board games or games such as scrabble, to help the child to become more familiar with words and reading in general.

Spelling

Spelling can be a long-term difficulty for children with dyslexia. Accurate spelling requires good short- and long-term memory skills, skills in placing letters in the correct sequence, accurate listening to detect the sounds in words and the ability to remember spelling rules and the groups of letters that make up specific sounds, such as 'ch' and 'sh'. These factors can be quite challenging for children with dyslexia. Moreover, once a child begins to misspell a word habitually, it will become almost ingrained and the child will misspell the word automatically. It is difficult to reverse this trend when the child has reached that stage. It is clearly better to deal with spelling difficulties as early as possible, but it is still very difficult even if this is done to help dyslexic children to remember and utilise spelling rules. When a child is writing a piece of information, the writing process – that is, the content and the language expression – may take precedence over spelling. The child is too 'busy' concentrating on what he or she is writing to think about correct spelling. It is important, therefore, that time and opportunities are available for proof-reading. Even proof-reading or checking one's work can be difficult, but the extra few minutes doing this can pay dividends, especially for dyslexic students in secondary school. It is best to check once for meaning and a second time for accuracy of spelling.

It is also a good idea for children or young adults with dyslexia to develop their own notebook of words that they usually misspell. They will then know which words to concentrate on when checking their spelling.

TextHelp©

The use of a word processor with a good spell-checker is of great benefit. Some spell-checkers may not identify some of the errors made by dyslexic children because the spelling does not resemble the actual word accurately enough. A spell-checker such as TextHelp© is superb because it is specially designed to identify dyslexic spelling errors.

TextHelp© is particularly useful for assisting with essay writing. It has a read-back facility and a spell-checker that includes a dyslexic spell-check option that searches for common dyslexic errors. Additionally, TextHelp© has a word prediction feature that can predict the meaning of a word from the context of the sentence, giving up to 10 options from a drop-down menu. Dyslexic students often have difficulty in finding the correct word and this feature can therefore be very useful. The software also has a 'word wizard' that provides the user with a definition of any word; options regarding homophones; an outline of a phonic map; and a talking help file.

Look, cover, write and check

This procedure is used at school to help to develop spelling accuracy. Basically it involves a number of stages that the child can adopt to obtain accuracy in spelling. Firstly, the child looks at the word so that he or she will have a visual image of it; the word is then covered over and the child writes it and finally checks if it has been spelled accurately.

This process can promote visual learning of words. Additionally, even if the word is not spelled correctly, the child will have the opportunity to self-correct and this, in itself, can help to develop accuracy in spelling.

Writing

Writing, such as creative writing, can be very frustrating for children with dyslexia. It is also frustrating for parents who know that their child is capable of performing at a higher level. Usually there is a discrepancy between the child's written performance and his or her knowledge of the subject. Children with dyslexia do not usually perform to their best in written form, which is unfortunate and frustrating. Certainly parents can help to encourage their child to write, and although word-processing can help this process considerably, some support is also necessary. Many teachers now realise that children with dyslexia need structure and cues to help to develop their writing and generate ideas. Structure words can be used, such as:

- when
- where
- people
- sound
- colour
- background.

These words can prompt ideas and generate a fuller piece of work.

Another method of helping with writing that is used in schools – and can also be used by parents – is the idea of writing frames. David Wray, from the University of Warwick, has developed a number of examples using writing frames. Writing frames can help with the aspects of creative writing, as shown in Figure 3.1.

Writing frames can therefore be used as a guide by parents if the child becomes frustrated in a writing exercise.

One of the key factors in relation to writing is confidence. Unfortunately children with dyslexia may not have much confidence in writing or, indeed, in learning. Therefore, boosting the self-esteem of the child with dyslexia is very important.

Self-esteem

Self-esteem is without doubt one of the influential factors in successful learning. Parents need to look for ways of boosting their child's

---

Argument

I think that _____ because _____.
The reasons for my thinking this are, firstly _____.
Another reason is _____.
Moreover _____ because _____.
These (facts / arguments / ideas) show that _____.
Some people think that _____ because _____
   they argue that _____.

Discussion

Another group who agree with this point of view are _____.
They say that _____.
On the other hand _____ disagree _____
   with the idea that _____.
They claim that _____.
They also say _____.
My opinion is _____
   because _____.

Figure 3.1 Writing frames. Adapted from David Wray's website: http://www.warwick.ac.uk/staff/D.J.Wray/Ideas/frames.html

self-esteem, and some suggestions are presented below:

- **Praise** – This is fairly obvious, but it is important that praise is also given for what the child has *attempted* and not only for what he or she has *completed*. It may be necessary for parents to readjust their perceptions of success, but at the same time keep in mind that the child very likely has abilities that are not being displayed. This can be frustrating and annoying for parents and progress can be slower than hoped, but it is important that praise is given for the child's attempts at the work.

- **Avoid comparison with others** – It is important not to compare your child with others. Children progress at different rates in different ways, so it is important to hold the individuality of your child in high regard and ensure that your child realises this. A secure child will learn more effectively and have a more positive self-concept than a child who is anxious.

- **Encourage peer friendships and clubs outwith school** – Many children with dyslexia receive a considerable boost to their self-esteem through success in outside school activities.

- **Try to limit time spent on homework** – If your child is spending too much time on homework, it might be wise to discuss this with the school. Pouring over homework for hours can be frustrating and this may reduce the time the child can spend on other activities that may bring him or her more success, such as participation in sport.
- **Try to work out your child's learning style** – The school may help in this respect. Learning styles are discussed below and you will note that children usually work more effectively if they can recognise and use their own learning styles. This can be visual, auditory, kinaesthetic or tactile, but environmental factors such as sound, light, time of day and even seating arrangements can make a difference.
- **Work positively with the school** – This is important. If parent/school cooperation is absent, the child will sense it and may feel that he or she is the problem. This can have an adverse affect on the child's self-esteem.

Learning styles

It is important that children are aware of their learning preferences. The acquisition of a successful learning style is an important determinant of successful learning – irrespective of the task, or the material to be learned. Learning styles are certainly important at school but it is also significant that parents recognise their child's learning style and learning preferences at home. Children may have different learning styles from their parents and parents should appreciate the different ways in which their children can learn.

A questionnaire, known as the Learning Styles Inventory (see Dunn et al., 1989), is used in some schools to help teachers to identify learning styles. An outline of this inventory is described below as it can give parents an overview of the different areas and factors that can contribute to learning styles.

The inventory contains 104 items that produce a profile of learning style preferences in five different areas: environmental, emotional, sociological, physiological and psychological. Within these areas, 21 different factors are seen to be important. These are:

- environmental (sound, light, temperature, design)
- emotional (motivation, persistence, responsibility, structure)
- sociological (learning by self, pairs, peers, team, with an adult)

- physiological (perceptual preference, food and drink intake, time of day, mobility)
- psychological (global preferences, analytic preferences, impulsive and reflective).

Research by Dunn and Dunn (1992, 1993) suggests that learning styles make a difference and all the above areas need to be focused on at some point. This can have implications for how your child studies at home.

Based on the above factors, Given and Reid (1999) developed a framework for observing learning styles – the Interactive Observational Style Identification (IOSI). Although the aim of the IOSI is to help teachers to recognise different learning styles, it can also be useful for parents because, again, it can create an awareness of the different areas that can contribute to learning styles.

The learning styles in the IOSI system are:

- *Motivation*
  - What topics, tasks and activities interest the child?
  - What kind of prompting and cueing is necessary to increase motivation?
  - What kind of incentives motivate the child: leadership opportunities, working with others, free time or physical activity?

- *Persistence*
  - Does the child stick to a task until completion without breaks?
  - Are frequent breaks necessary when working on difficult tasks?

- *Responsibility*
  - To what extent does the child take responsibility for his or her own learning?
  - Does the child attribute success or failure to self or others?

- *Structure*
  - Are the child's personal effects (desk, clothing, materials) well organised or cluttered?
  - How does the child respond to someone imposing an organisational structure on him or her?

- *Interaction*
  - Is the child's best work accomplished when working alone, with another person, or in a small group?

– Does the child ask for approval or does his or her work need to be checked frequently?

- *Communication*
  – Does the child give the main events and gloss over the details?
  – Does the child interrupt when others are talking?

- *Modality preference*
  – What type of instructions does the child most easily understand? Written, oral or visual?
  – Does the child respond more quickly and easily to questions about stories heard or read?
  – Does the child begin with one step and proceed in an orderly fashion or does he or she have difficulty following sequential information?
  – Is there a logical sequence to the child's explanations or do his or her thoughts jump from one idea to another?

- *Impulsive/reflective*
  – Are the child's responses rapid and spontaneous or are they delayed and reflective?
  – Does the child seem to consider past events before taking action?

- *Mobility*
  – Does the child move around the class a lot or fidget when seated?
  – Does the child like to stand or walk while learning something new?

- *Food intake*
  – Does the child snack or chew on a pencil when studying?

- *Time of day*
  – During which time of day is the child most alert?
  – Is there a noticeable difference between work completed in the morning and work completed in the afternoon?

- *Sound*
  – Does the child seek out places that are particularly quiet?

- *Light*
  – Does the child like to work in dimly lit areas or say that the light is too bright?

- *Temperature*
  - Does the child leave his or her coat on when others seem to be comfortable without a coat?

- *Furniture design*
  - When given a choice, does the child sit on the floor, lie down or sit in a straight chair to read?

- *Metacognition*
  - Is the child aware of the strengths of his or her learning style?
  - Does the child demonstrate self-assessment?

- *Prediction*
  - Does the child make plans and work towards goals or let things happen?

- *Feedback*
  - How does the child respond to different types of feedback?
  - How much external prompting is needed before the child can access previous knowledge?

The main point of the above is that virtually all factors within the child and within the environment, as well as factors relating to the task, can impinge on learning styles. It may be necessary to observe children as they go about their everyday lives at home. Do they have preferences for seating arrangements, for writing, for reading and are they more awake in the morning or in the evening? By watching and also asking a child it is possible to find out something about his or her learning preferences. Once you have an idea of the child's preferences you may then have to make some accommodation to help to promote more effective learning through the child's learning style.

Summary

This chapter has provided insights on how children learn and has given some suggestions on how parents may supplement the work being carried out in school. Some of the key points mentioned in this chapter include:

- Information processing, i.e. how children with dyslexia process information – that is, how they take in information, understand it and retain it for future use.
- Memory skills: how information can be organised to enhance retention, the implications of this for remembering school time-tables and organising written work.
- Strategies that can be carried out at home to develop reading, spelling and creative writing.
- Self-esteem and the importance of a positive self-concept for learning.
- Learning styles and how parents can help to identify their child's learning preferences. Although this has implications for the school, it also has implications for the home. It is important that children with dyslexia are aware of their learning style as this can help them to learn independently. This also gives the child some responsibility for learning, which is commendable and fits in with the trend towards self-advocacy. It is important that children and young people with dyslexia should take control of their own learning at some point and be aware of how they can learn most effectively.

Chapter 4

Support for parents

The following scenario is very common:

The parents have been concerned with the progress of their child. He or she is reaching a reasonable level of attainments but they suspect that this level is below the child's potential and abilities. They decide to go for a formal assessment. This can be carried out through the school or independently. The assessment takes place and the results indicate dyslexia. How do the parents react to this? Immediately they try to seek out information on dyslexia – they may feel confused, anxious and perhaps alone.

The above situation, and the immediate reaction of anxiety when parents discover that their child has dyslexia, occurs frequently. It is, however, important that parents are given avenues of support as soon as dyslexia is diagnosed, as this can prevent some of the questions and anxieties that can sometimes follow a diagnosis of dyslexia. Certainly if the assessment is carried out independently of the school, then the first avenue of support should be the school. If the assessment is carried out in school, then support should be provided automatically. Many assessments for dyslexia, however, are carried out independently by a chartered and experienced educational psychologist. Irrespective of how the diagnosis is conducted, the first line of communication should always be the school.

Communication with the school

When schools and parents work in harmony the outcome is always more profitable for the child. If the assessment is carried out independently the parents should make an appointment to discuss the report with the school as soon as possible. It is possible that the school will have a different perspective from the psychologist who conducted the assessment, but this should not matter. A diagnosis is important as it can provide a reason for the difficulties the child is experiencing in school and a way forward for both the child and the parents. The descriptive characteristics of the child's profile that can emerge from an assessment are also important – that is, the child's strengths and difficulties. These can be considered by the school and acted on. At the same time a diagnosis of dyslexia would imply that the child will require some special consideration, quite apart from that which may normally be offered by the school. The important point is that communication of some sort needs to take place.

Questions that parents may want to ask the school

- How does my child get along with others?
- Does my child participate well in group activities?
- What can I do at home to encourage or help my child to learn to read, spell and write?
- Can you describe my child's reading programme?
- How does the dyslexic difficulties my child is experiencing affect him or her in the classroom?
- How can we help to overcome these difficulties?
- What kind of changes will the school make to my child's literacy programmes in the light of the diagnosis of dyslexia?
- To what extent will the dyslexic difficulties my child is experiencing hinder him or her in the future?

These questions should be answered by the school and it is therefore important to arrange a meeting at the school as soon as possible after a diagnosis of dyslexia.

Meetings at school

As indicated above, arranging a meeting with the school is crucial and this should be done as soon as possible after the assessment is carried out. For some parents a school meeting can be an anxious time. One of the best ways to try to minimise the anxiety is to have a set of questions ready so that you know what **you** want to get out of the meeting. It might also be a good idea if you can tell the school the general areas you want to discuss prior to the meeting, and to find out who will be present at the meeting. This will avoid an unexpected surprise when you enter the meeting room and find a group of professionals sitting round a table all prepared to discuss your child with you. This is quite possible as there can be quite a range of professionals involved in your child's education, particularly if he or she is experiencing some difficulties. For example, Table 4.1 lists the people who may be involved and the extent of their potential involvement.

Table 4.1 Professionals and their involvement

Professional	Potential involvement
Class teacher	He or she should be able to discuss your child's day-to-day class progress, the areas of strength and difficulties experienced and how these are being addressed. Also, how your child performs within the class in relation to interaction with others, motivation and general well-being
Support teacher	The support teacher can have a range of titles depending on the system used in the education authority and the country. For example: in England the title can be SENCO (Special Educational Needs Coordinator); in Scotland, Support For Learning; in the

Continues

Table 4.1 *Continues*

Professional	Potential involvement
	USA, resource teachers; in New Zealand, RTLB (Resource Teacher Learning and Behaviour). These are just examples but there will likely be someone in the school who is trained to deal with reading difficulties or specific difficulties for dyslexia. This person should be able to provide specialist advice and his or her role may be to advise the class teacher and provide some advice on any specialist programme that parents can readily use to complement what is going on in school
Head teacher	The head teacher would normally chair the meeting and welcome the parents. The head will be responsible for ensuring that the parents' questions have been answered and for making a record of the meeting. If it is not possible for the head to be present it is likely that he or she will appoint a deputy replacement
Educational psychologist	The educational psychologist is often the person responsible for the assessment and, if appropriate, any diagnosis. He or she will provide a profile of the child's strengths and weaknesses and provide some suggestions for the parents and the school. In the UK most educational psychologists are chartered and a member of the British Psychological Society
Classroom assistant	In some situations there may be a classroom assistant and it may be appropriate if he or she joins the meeting. Often the classroom assistant will have the duty of carrying out a programme with the child or spending some time with him or her in class
Speech and language therapist	In some cases a speech therapist may attend the meeting, particularly if the child is very young and there are speech and language difficulties for which the child is obtaining some support

Professional	Potential involvement
Occupational therapist	The occupational therapist will be useful if there are coordination and balance difficulties and problems associated with writing and movement skills, such as clumsiness and spatial difficulties
Educational adviser	If there is some doubt about provision and perhaps a change of school may be a possible outcome, an educational adviser representing the education authority may be present. Some advisers may also have specialist knowledge in dyslexia
Other professional	Depending on the type of difficulties the child displays, other professionals may be present at the meeting. For example, occupational therapists are increasingly being involved in intervention programmes. They can advise on a programme involving motor and movement difficulties

As can be seen from Table 4.1, the range of professionals who may be involved can be quite varied. At some meetings, of course, it may only be necessary for the class teacher to be present. This can be quite an informal meeting, but there is no reason why larger meetings should not also be informal. It is important that parents are not intimidated by being faced with an array of professionals. Professionals have the interests of the child at heart and it is important that meetings are conducted in a congenial and collaborative atmosphere.

Pre-meeting pointers for parents

- Identify the purpose for the meeting.
- Plan for the meeting. Write out the areas and questions you want the meeting to cover. You may want to prioritise these questions in case time does not allow you to cover them all.

- Restate or make sure that the person who is chairing the meeting restates the purpose of the meeting at the onset This is important as it ensures that all those present will know the purpose of the meeting.
- Try to keep to one topic since the length of the meeting will be limited. If the class teacher is present, class cover may have to be organised, and it will be disappointing and very frustrating if the meeting ends with many questions still unanswered.
- Display a positive attitude during the conference. Be aware that not only what you say reflects your attitude, but also your tone of voice and your facial expressions. Body movements can also be important. A loud voice may imply dominance. Rigid posture may suggest anger or disapproval.
- Do not be overawed by the number or experience of the professionals who may be at the meeting. I still recall attending such a meeting when my son was very young. Within minutes of the meeting starting I scanned around the table, counted the number of professionals and felt quite humbled that all those people had made an effort to attend the meeting to suit my convenience for the benefit of my son. While this was true, and I as a parent was appreciative, it did overawe me slightly with the result that I was not able to ask the type of questions I wanted to.
- Show yourself to be open and supportive throughout the meeting. Don't become antagonistic or defensive otherwise the meeting can become a negative experience for all. Even if an unfortunate comment is made, try to remain calm and objective. This can be difficult for you, especially since it is your child. His or her welfare and education are obviously very important to you and to the professionals, but it is also important that the relations between you and the school are harmonious.
- Try to ensure that suggestions are made that will increase your child's opportunities for learning. Try to ensure that provision has been made not only for the short-term but also for the long-term success and progress.
- Ask for examples of your child's work to be brought to the meeting. This will help you to note progress at future meetings when samples of work will also be shown.
- Either you, or the person chairing the meeting, should clarify and summarise each important point as it is discussed, and sum up at the

end. If the chairperson does not do this you should request it, or do it yourself and take notes.

Support from organisations

Apart from obtaining help from school, there is a range of organisations that parents can contact for information and support if their child has been diagnosed as dyslexic. Most of these organisations can be found on the internet but many parents prefer some local and immediate contact. Furthermore, many parents want to speak with someone local, and usually sooner rather than later, so an immediate telephone contact is usually preferable. It is also possible for parents to become involved in the running of an organisation. Many new organisations are set up with charitable status, but there are quite a number of dyslexia organisations in most countries and these should be accessible by parents.

There is not the same amount of support groups for adults with dyslexia, but it may be possible for a group of adults to establish such a group locally.

Guidance in setting up a parent group

- Ensure that there is a core of volunteers who can offer their spare time, otherwise much of the work can fall on one or two individuals. If, for some reason, they leave the group – perhaps they are leaving the area – the group may be in danger of collapse.
- You will need to have a constitution outlining the procedures for the election and length of term of office bearers, financial auditing, AGMs, aims and purpose of the group.
- Financial support. There can be some overheads in setting up a group, such as stationery, premises and expenses, and fees to speakers who may be invited to come along to the meetings. There should also be opportunities and ideas for raising funds.
- Try to obtain the services of professionals such as a lawyer or an accountant who may have some connections with dyslexia and is prepared to provide services free of charge.
- A bank account with two authorised signatures will be necessary.

- Make contact with a high-ranking official in the education department to inform him or her about the establishment of the group and its purposes. It is better if officials from education hear about the group first hand rather than through some publicity for the group. Invite a key person from the education department to join the group, or the committee, or to talk to the group at one of its meetings.
- Have clear aims and a programme of events that reflect those aims (some suggested areas/ideas for speakers are given in the following section).
- A helpline is a good idea but it requires someone to be available during the helpline hours. It is better in the beginning to offer only a few hours several times a week to ensure that someone will always be available.
- Link with a larger national group if one is available. Many organisations, such as the British Dyslexia Association in the UK, the International Dyslexia Association in the USA and the SPELD groups in Australia and New Zealand, have many branches and a new group may consider being an affiliate of the main national group. In some countries, different groups that have been established for often the same reason do not seem to work in harmony with each other. This situation should be avoided at all costs as it can be confusing for parents and, indeed, for those working in the education department.

Suggested areas/ideas for speakers

Some suggestions for the type of speakers and areas that can be welcomed by other parents are given below:

- Education adviser for the local area – to discuss the authority's provision for dyslexia.
- Educational psychologist – to discuss how children are identified and assessed.
- Specialist teacher with qualifications in dyslexia – to indicate any specific approaches/programmes that can be used by parents.
- Speech and language therapists – to discuss their role identification, assessment and intervention in relation to dyslexia and, perhaps, other specific learning difficulties.

- Occupational therapists – to discuss the connections between motor/movement and dyslexia and perhaps to suggest some activities that the parents can do at home.
- Academics – to provide an overview of some of the recent research in dyslexia.
- Authors of books for children – some authors may have a special interest in dyslexia. Some publishers commission books that are dyslexia-friendly, have high interest levels, but a lower level of vocabulary to enable the child with dyslexia to read the text fluently and with interest. One such company in the UK is Barrington Stoke (see Chapter 9), who now have a very comprehensive catalogue of children's books especially designed for the reluctant reader.
- Innovations and alternative interventions – there are a number of alternative interventions that have been suggested for dyslexia (see Chapter 8). It is a good idea to invite speakers to talk on these issues and invite teachers from the local schools. Some current interventions that may be relevant include: DDAT (Dyslexia, Dyspraxia and Attention Treatment); coloured lenses; brain gym; dietary items such as essential fatty acid supplements; speakers representing organisations with programmes/strategies that are used for dyslexia, such as Mind Mapping©; Buzan centres; the Davis orientation method; the Fast Forward phonics programme.
- Parents – to talk about their experiences and the strategies they use at home.
- Adults with dyslexia – to talk about their challenges and how these have been overcome.
- Representatives of universities and colleges – to discuss the arrangements that can be made for dyslexic students.
- Careers personnel – to discuss employment opportunities.
- Employers – to talk about the accommodation that can be made for adults with dyslexia.

What can organisations provide?

Organisations can provide a considerable amount of support to parents, especially parents who have only recently found out that their child is dyslexic and require some guidance. Organisations can provide:

- Information about dyslexia.
- Contact with other parents.
- Regular meetings to hear speakers talk about different aspects of dyslexia.
- Opportunities to team up with parents from the same school as your child who also have a dyslexic child.
- Information on the legislation relating to dyslexia and particularly the rights of parents and children.
- Information on psychological assessments.
- Links with other organisations.
- Lobbying and negotiating platforms.

Chapter 9 contains some websites where national organisations for a number of different countries can be found. These can provide a link to local information and organisations.

Working at home with your child

It is important that undue pressure is not put on the child at home. This is easier said than done as homework can sometimes take the child with dyslexia twice as long to complete. This, of course, can put pressure on the child, and it is not fair that school work should totally absorb the child's leisure time. If this happens it would be wise for the parents to talk to the teacher and some consideration may be given to this issue by the school.

Essentially home can be a refuge for children with dyslexia, and it is important that the child does not experience additional pressures from well-meaning but anxious parents. This can be difficult as parents, rightly so, want the best for their child and achievements at school are important to secure a place on college or university courses as well as employment in an increasingly competitive employment market.

Some guidance to parents on the issue of working at home with a child is shown below:

- Consider what would be an adequate length of time to spend on homework and ensure that your child is not spending more time than he or she should.
- Discuss any issues arising from the length of time spent on homework with the school.

- Discuss the homework with your child before he or she starts it. A parent can help the child to establish exactly what has to be done and the materials that will be necessary.
- Ensure that the homework is carried out in an environment that suits your child's learning styles. If some background music is required, then allow this as it may help your child to concentrate.
- Discuss the homework with your child when it has been completed and discuss the comments made by the teacher on the homework after it has been seen by the teacher.
- Ensure that there is a balance in your child's out-of-school time between school work and free time.
- Extra tuition can sometimes be helpful, but it is important that any tuition independent of the school should in some way link with school work, otherwise it could be counter-productive.
- Remember that some television programmes can be educational, so do not unduly restrict this although, clearly, television should be used in moderation. Similarly, learning through the internet can be very educational but it is only one means of obtaining information. Television and learning through the internet, however, can become a family activity or at least two members of the family can be involved.
- Try to ensure that the child sees learning as fun. The internet can help to achieve that and children with dyslexia often prefer exploratory and investigative learning to remembering information and facts.

Choosing a dyslexia-friendly school

There are a number of issues about the choice of school. In some cases parents may not have any choice, but if there is a choice, parents should find out how the school deals with dyslexia and make a decision based on that information. Clearly there are a number of questions that parents may want to ask, including:

- Does the school have any teachers who hold a recognised qualification for teaching children with dyslexia?
- Does the school have any special provision for dyslexic children – units, facilities for one-to-one tuition, school–parent programmes?
- What is the average class size? This can make a difference. Children with dyslexia may become 'lost' if classes are too large and their

needs may be inadvertently ignored because they appear to be coping. In a small class they cannot 'hide' to the same extent.
- Does the school have any obvious dyslexia-friendly policies and practices? The term dyslexia-friendly is a useful one. Some of the features of dyslexia-friendly schools are shown below.

Dyslexia–friendly schools: what are they?

Neil Mackay (2004) first coined the phrase dyslexia-friendly schools while involved with schools in North Wales throughout the 1990s. He describes the process that was used in Clwyd Education Authority (now Flintshire) in the establishment of a dyslexia resource within the school. The children received five hours of small group specialist tuition and spent the rest of their time in mainstream classes. Since these children would be spending 20 hours each week with mainstream subject specialists, training sessions were organised on dyslexia awareness, strategies for supporting literacy, learning skills and numeracy. Mackay (2004) describes how Swansea Local Education Authority adopted the idea and developed it from a whole school approach into a celebrated strategy across all schools in the authority.

Mackay also describes the ideal school for dealing with dyslexia and helping dyslexic children. This school:

- recognises that all children learn in different ways;
- helps children to utilise their own individual learning styles;
- recognises that many apparent learning difficulties can often be explained as leaning differences and that these will respond to changes in methods, materials and approaches;
- is particularly aware of the needs of the growing numbers of non-traditional learners who do not function well in some learning environments;
- encourages children to explore ideas, concepts and strategies within the framework of their preferred learning styles;
- is very successful in terms of results, but it values this success less than it values the confident and independent learners it is developing;
- seeks to empower all pupils to be the best they can be;
- sees parents as partners;

- enjoys the trust of parents; and
- is not only dyslexia-friendly but also learning friendly.

There are a growing number of schools in both the state and independent sector that fulfil or strive to fulfil the spirit of dyslexia-friendliness in school. Much can be learned from examining the practice and organisation in good and effective dyslexia-friendly schools. Schools that exist only for children with dyslexia can, in many cases, offer an educational experience not available in mainstream schools. Some parents and children, of course, may prefer to attend a mainstream school, and that is their entitlement; it is also their entitlement that their educational needs are met and it is often a case of striking a balance between a number of factors to obtain this. For example, the child may have to travel further to school and may have to temporarily leave the mainstream school for a short period. It is possible for separate and independent provision to be viewed within the education authority's policy and package for inclusive schools.

Inclusion

'Inclusion' is a term now widely used in education. It centres on social and educational equality and it is hypothesised that mainstream schools should play a major role in achieving this for all children. Of course they should but, as all parents know, every child is different and therefore each child will have a different set of needs. These differences need to be acknowledged and accommodation made for them in schools. This, in fact, has presented challenges to the education system since the Education Act (1994). The 1944 Act responded to this challenge by imposing a system of selection and segregation that, in fact, failed many children.

The current legislation in most countries, which is discussed in the next chapter, attempts to provide equality through access to a full and balanced curriculum – the very essence of inclusion. In England there is a national inclusion statement which includes a section on responding to pupils' diverse needs. This states that teachers should take action to respond to pupils' diverse needs by:

- creating effective learning environments
- securing children's motivation and concentration

- providing equality of opportunity through teaching approaches
- setting targets for learning.

As these factors will require considerable time and effort before they are fully implemented into practice, there will inevitably be variations in how this is achieved in different parts of the country.

An effective education for your child with dyslexia is a balance between social inclusion, which ensures that he or she is part of a positive friendship grouping, and educational outcomes, which can ensure that your child reaches his or her full potential. The actual means, resources and provision to achieve this can be different for different children. Inclusion should certainly be seen as a desirable product, but there are a number of routes to achieve this.

As part of the research for this book I interviewed a head teacher of a school for children with dyslexia (the Red Rose School in St Anne's on Sea in Lancashire, UK). I asked her how inclusive small schools, such as the Red Rose School, are – particularly as they only cater for children with dyslexia? She indicated that small schools such as hers can be very inclusive and actually embrace the community to participate in school activities. She also indicated that the children at the Red Rose School attend for a relatively short period of time before they return to the mainstream school or to college. During their time at the school they develop the confidence and acquire the literacy skills that enable them to return to the mainstream and constructively participate in the mainstream curriculum, therefore benefiting from an inclusive education. Without the intensive and short-term support of the small dedicated provision, they would not have otherwise been able to access the curriculum and would have been essentially excluded.

One of the key aspects to your child having full and fair curriculum access is to be aware of what schools need to provide and to be able to communicate with the school. Parents should feel familiar with the school and be able to find their way around the school. Some suggestions that parents may make to schools include:

- Clear instructions on how the class teacher can be contacted and when.
- Clear signs so that parents can navigate around the school comfortably.

- A set time when parents are welcome to visit the school.
- Provision for working parents on how they may contact the school.
- Open evenings that are at a time and day suitable for most parents.
- Home–school notebooks that can be very helpful for working parents.

It is also worth considering that parents of dyslexic children may also be dyslexic themselves, and this may have an impact on how parents can be used supportively.

Self-advocacy

There is a growing trend towards self-advocacy in education and in society. This means that children, young adults and parents need to be aware of their rights and be able to speak up for these rights. But it also means that schools should help to equip children with the ability to speak for themselves. This will be a skill that will benefit them in later life and particularly in the workplace. Parents also have a role to play in assisting their child in self-advocacy skills. Perhaps one of the best pieces of advice parents can give their child is to communicate. It is too easy for children who are experiencing any type of difficulty in school to keep it to themselves or 'bottle it up' to such an extent that it is released in the form of unacceptable, inappropriate and sometimes explosive behaviour.

Certainly it is not always possible in the case of very young children to be a self-advocate, but at least if the child is able to communicate what is affecting him or her to a teacher or parent, then that in itself will help to provide a solution.

The difficulty for parents, of course, is that often the child finds it difficult to identify exactly what is going wrong and why. Even at the best of times parenting can be a challenging duty. Parents have to be, at the same time, disciplinarians and councillors. It is a question of balance, but there is no doubt that very often children with dyslexia will respond more to the counselling approach. Some suggestions for parents on counselling children with dyslexia include:

- Self-esteem – It has been reiterated a number of times in this book that self-esteem is important and the child with a positive self-esteem will open up and be more likely to discuss any problems than a child with a negative self-esteem. It is important, therefore, to make the child feel good and that can clear the way for the discussion of any difficulties.

- Make a space for family or parent–child discussion. If this happens on a regular basis, even when the child is not experiencing any obvious problems, it will set a pattern of discussion, and if a problem does occur, it can be discussed in the normal pattern of family discussions.
- Try not to show the child any anxieties you may have because they will soon be felt by the child and make it less likely that he or she will want to discuss them.
- Listen and have faith in your child's views and what he or she wants to do.
- Ask questions about what the child says to you, not what you want to say to the child. Let the child take the lead.
- At the end of the discussion try to agree on some course of action – even if it is just to discuss the same issue the following week. Never leave it to drift.
- Take what your child says seriously. This may seem obvious, but even if the child raises what seems to be a trivial matter, it will be a major issue to him or her and needs to be taken seriously.
- Involve the family, if appropriate, as this can help to normalise the issue as everyone in the family, dyslexic or not, will experience some problems and difficulties. The dyslexic difficulties will then just be a variation in the normal course of family discussion.
- Inform the school if your child raises any issue. That is not the same as complaining to the school, but rather communicating with the school so that all involved with the child have the same knowledge. Of course, you first need to suggest to your child that the school should know.
- Avoid confrontation, as this will put up barriers that will, in fact, prevent free and relaxed discussion and make any counselling or supportive discussion impossible.
- Praise and thank your child for discussing this with you. This will make it easier for him or her to discuss any issues with you in the future.

While, as indicated above, there is a trend towards self-advocacy, it is not always easy to put this into practice. Authority is still authority and this can represent fear rather than freedom to many – both children and adults. It is important, therefore, that parents have some knowledge of their legal rights. This is discussed in the next chapter.

Summary

This chapter has focused on the range of support that can be utilised by parents. Some of this support can be in the form of self-help but one of the key aspects relates to communication, particularly with the school.

The chapter has given some outline guidance on:

- Questions that parents may want to ask the school.
- Pre-meeting preparation prior to a school meeting.
- The range and type of supports that can be available from organisations.
- Guidance in setting up a parent group.
- Dyslexia organisations and websites.
- Working at home with your child.
- Choosing a dyslexia-friendly school.
- Self-advocacy.

The points discussed in this chapter can provide some guidance to parents. There is certainly much support and potential areas of support available, but even with the best form of support the emotional and psychological demands of helping to maintain the child's self-esteem and the motivation of the child with dyslexia can be significant. At the same time there are a great many success stories. Young people with dyslexia can achieve considerable success at college, the workplace and in society, and such examples of success can give enormous hope to parents.

Chapter 5

Legislation and parent empowerment

Equity and education

Since the Salamanca Statement (1994) there has been a considerable thrust towards equality in education throughout Europe. This trend has also been noted throughout the world and there are similarities in educational philosophies – principally relating to inclusion, parental involvement, equity and student advocacy in the USA, Canada, Australia, New Zealand and throughout Europe.

The Salamanca Statement (UNESCO, 1994) paved a powerful path on the road to educational equality and inclusive policies. The statement indicated that

> schools should accommodate to all children regardless of their physical, intellectual, social, emotional, linguistic or other conditions.... Many children experience learning difficulties and thus have special educational needs at some time during their schooling.... Schools have to find ways of successfully educating all children, including those who have serious disadvantages and disabilities ... emerging consensus that children with special educational needs should be included in the educational arrangements made for the majority of children. This has led to the concept of the inclusive school.
>
> (UNESCO, 1994)

This kind of statement has certainly provided motivation for governments to reform education systems, but at the same time implementing this in practice is quite another matter. Many dyslexia support groups in different countries, although they applaud the desire of governments to meet the needs of all children, still harbour concerns on current legislation and legislative reforms. For example, the IDA has issued policy statements on a number of Acts in the USA, such as the Full Funding of the Individuals with Disabilities Education Act (2001a) and the Reauthorization of the Elementary and Secondary Education Act (2001b). Both these IDA statements are strong in tone and talk direct to the government. For example, in relation to the Individuals with Disabilities Act (IDEA) the IDA stated that:

> the IDA favors increases that will lead to the full funding of IDEA. It is essential that, in addition to higher funding for state grants, discretionary programs receive adequate funding so that they can provide a stronger infrastructure for basic services. . . . We recognize that there are budget constraints that require phasing in higher funding over a number of years and we oppose any policies and procedures that would increase special education funding at the expense of regular education. We will be happy to work with Congress and other interested education and disability organizations in developing approaches that will lead to full funding in ways that are beneficial to the entire US educational system.
>
> (IDA policy statement www.interdys.org)

This clearly indicates the scope and potential of dyslexia associations such as the IDA. This chapter will also refer to examples from other countries that highlight the influence that voluntary associations can have on governments.

England and Wales Code of Practice: implications for parents

One of the most important pieces of legislation in England and Wales in relation to meeting the needs of children with dyslexia is the revised Code of Practice (2001). The Code of Practice indicates that if a dyslexic child has needs that cannot adequately be met, there may be a requirement for a statement of educational need to be formulated in order to protect the child's interests.

The Code of Practice recognises that all parents of children with special educational needs should be treated as partners and should be empowered to play a full and active role in their child's education. This also means that the LEA will provide them with 'information, advice and support during assessment and any related decision-making process about special educational provision' (Code of Practice, para 2.2). One of the means of empowering parents in England and Wales throughout this process is the Parent Partnership Scheme (PPS) – see pages 97–99.

One of the outcomes of an assessment process could be the formulation of a statement of educational needs. A statement should clearly specify the provision necessary to meet each identified need. This means that provision should be quantified in terms of number of hours, staffing requirements and any specific programme or intervention required. This can be achieved through the introduction of an Individual Educational Plan (IEP), and parents should be consulted throughout its development. Depending on the age of the child, he or she should be involved in the planning of an IEP. The system involves a graduated process of assessing the child's needs; therefore, before a statement is considered, the process of 'school action' and 'school action plus' has to be applied. These stages place considerable onus on schools to provide for the child to meet his or her needs.

The original Code of Practice (1994) provided for a five-stage assessment process with the first stage highlighting a 'cause for concern'. The revised code indicates that all children should be monitored and their needs catered for within the practice of inclusion. Differentiation is therefore seen as an implicit and fundamental component of classroom practice. This means that teaching approaches and learning materials have to be 'differentiated' to ensure that all children have full access to the curriculum. Differentiation is not only about ensuring that the content of lessons and worksheets and books have a range of tasks, and that the vocabulary used incorporates a range of reading levels, but it is also about how lessons are taught and presented to children in the classroom situation. This places a considerable responsibility on teachers. Parents need to be sure that their child is receiving some type of differentiation, if that is seen to be appropriate. This can be the focus of discussions with the teacher.

The Code is, in fact, quite clear on the strands of differentiation. It indicates that teachers need to consider differentiation in relation to assessment, planning, reviewing, grouping for teaching purposes, additional support if appropriate, the curriculum and teaching methods.

Special Educational Needs and Disability Act

The Code of Practice is part of the Special Educational Needs and Disability Act (2001) – SENDA. This Act is an amended form of the Disability Discrimination Act (1995) (DDA) that was revised to cover education. The Act provides greater powers to the Special Educational Needs Tribunal and places a duty on LEAs to provide and advertise both a PPS and conciliation arrangements.

'Disability' and 'discrimination' are key words in the Act. The Act states that schools cannot discriminate against disabled pupils (the definition of 'disability' is very broad and dyslexia can be seen in terms of the Act as a disability) in all aspects of school life, including extra-curricular activities and school excursions.

Parents can claim unlawful discrimination by putting a case to a Special Educational Needs and Disability Tribunal. Under the Act it is unlawful for schools to discriminate in admissions and exclusions and a school cannot deliberately refuse an application from a disabled person for admission to the school. Discrimination is evident when a pupil is treated less favourably and may be at a disadvantage because the school has not made 'reasonable adjustments'. What is meant by 'reasonable' is not explicitly defined in the Act as this depends on individual cases and can be a matter for the tribunal or an appeal panel to decide.

Essentially the Act aims to incorporate parents as partners in the education of their child. This, of course, is very important in relation to children with special educational needs and parents should be informed when special education needs provision is made for their child.

Parent Partnership Schemes

In England and Wales LEAs are required to set up Parent Partnership Schemes (PPSs) on a statutory basis, although there are no national standards set. The aim of a PPS is to provide a range of services for parents whose children have a special educational need (SEN) so that parents can play an active and informed role in their child's education. This implies that if parents are consulted and their views are valued, then the education experience for the child, the parents and the school would be more harmonious and meaningful.

Nigel Pugh, who is a Parent Partnership Officer for Wiltshire LEA in England, suggests that PPSs have received a mixed reception, with some LEAs embracing the idea and others being less enthusiastic (Pugh, 2003). The involvement of the LEA, according to Pugh, can vary from merely offering a signposting service to other service providers to allowing PPS staff to support parents throughout the tribunal system, even if the tribunal complaint was against the LEA. The Department for Education and Science (DfES) laid out core activities for the PPSs. These include the need to:

- be able to work collaboratively with parents;
- provide information and other forms of publicity to parents;
- provide training advice and support to parents as appropriate;
- help parents to inform and influence local SEN policy and practice.

A PPS can also recruit and train an Independent Parental Supporter (IPS). The IPS is a volunteer and is independent of decision-making professionals. This, of course, means that there is no conflict of interest that one might find with LEA employees who may also be advising parents. The IPS can:

- provide advice to parents in their dealings with LEAs, schools and the SEN Tribunal;
- assist parents throughout the assessment process;
- help parents to understand the implications of any objectives set out in the statement that may result from the assessment; and
- discuss with parents the different options available to them in relation to the provision of their child's education.

A good example of the PPS in action is the SNAP Cymru Independent Parental Support Service in Wales (www.snapcymru.org). SNAP Cymru works directly with families, local authorities and the Welsh Assembly and provides a conciliatory service through local projects that try to ensure partnership in decision making at the earliest stage. By doing this it is hoped that potential conflicts can be avoided.

SNAP Cymru has responded to documents issued by the Welsh Assembly, worked collaboratively with schools and has supported community initiatives throughout Wales. One of its aims is to support parents in appeals against exclusion from school and in decisions made about their child's education. It therefore provides support for parent representation to pupil disciplinary committees, Independent Appeals Panels and the SEN Tribunal. One interesting and proactive aspect of the work of SNAP Cymru is the development of mediation services for disagreement resolution. This can result in free advice being offered to parents and to any other parties involved when an agreement has not been reached. This does not prejudice a family's right to access the SEN Tribunal, but does provide the opportunity for mediation that can prevent the necessity of a tribunal hearing.

Pugh (2003) suggests that PPSs have potentially a great deal to offer parents by helping them to understand the system and give them moral support when they may be at their most vulnerable. Pugh also suggests that a PPS can provide parents with the opportunity to directly influence their LEA's SEN policy if the PPS is properly managed. SNAP Cymru is a good example of this in practice. Pugh suggests that parents should ask LEAs questions such as who runs the service, who trains the IPS and what areas can the service not help with? (Information and updates on the above can be found on the DfES website – www.dfes.gov.uk.)

Legislation in Scotland

Scotland has had a long history of parents being able to access politicians, and since 1999, when the new Scottish Parliament was convened, this process has become easier with key politicians more accessible. Parents of children with dyslexia and parent groups have often been involved in discussions with education authorities and this has resulted in some good examples of collaboration. For example, in 1995 Fife Local Education Authority developed a policy for dyslexia called Partnership – Parents, Pupils and Professionals. This indicates the strong feeling of the need to engage parents as partners in education.

This view has also been noted in some other education authorities in Scotland, and many authorities (e.g. East Renfrewshire) have specifically included the parents in a number of areas of practice, such as early screening and in their multi-lingual policy. An audit of early years policy and provision for dyslexia (Reid et al., 2004) found that all education authorities in Scotland made provision for the involvement of parents in different stages of identification and intervention. Some excellent examples of good practice were noted. There were many examples of close liaison with parents at the pre-school stage.

The disability discrimination legislation passed by the UK government applies to Scotland, but not the Code of Practice and the areas associated with the Code. The Scottish Executive in April 2004 achieved agreement and passed the final stages of new legislation that will become law in September 2005. This legislation will have implications for special needs and for children with dyslexia and their parents. The legislation – Education (Additional Support for Learning) (Scotland) Bill – arose because it was felt that the existing assessment and recording system for children with SEN was outdated and too bureaucratic.

The aim of the legislation is to provide a framework that encompasses all children who may have difficulty in accessing and benefiting from learning, whatever the cause or reason for that difficulty. The legislation recognises that children are individuals and that some additional support needs are temporary, while others will present long-term barriers to effective learning. This provides the notion of educational support with a much wider framework than previously was the case.

Although parents will be able to formally request the education authority to establish whether their child has 'additional support needs', there are many concerns among parents that the impetus and emphasis previously placed on meeting the needs of some categories of learners, such as those with dyslexia, will be compromised.

One of the key aspects of the Bill is the formulating of Coordinated Support Plans (CSPs). These plans will replace the previous Record of Needs which, although they were appreciated by many parents, was a cumbersome and drawn-out procedure involving eight steps and the involvement of a number of professionals, as well as parents.

There is, however, some concern on the revised procedures on two counts. Firstly, a group of parents want to preserve the Record of Needs as they feel it gave them, and their child, some statutory protection and ensured some form of specialist provision and practice. Secondly, there are a number of concerns about the CSPs as the Bill indicates that children who have educational support needs **only** will **not** be eligible to be considered for a CSP. Only those children who have educational support needs and other support needs will be eligible to be considered for a CSP. The Bill does make reference to facilities such as 'Mediation Services' and 'Additional Support Needs Tribunals', but what is being contested by parent groups is the fact that the only matters that can be referred to a tribunal are those in connection with a CSP. If children with dyslexia do not have a CSP, then the parents will have no recourse to the tribunal system.

Dyslexia Scotland, the national parents support group, provided a written response during the consultation process of the Bill. They indicated that the Bill divides children with special needs, or additional support needs, into two classes: those who have legal rights and those who have not because they have educational support needs only.

On a more positive note, the Bill does require LEAs to identify and support children's needs including those under the age of 3, or not yet in nursery or school. This identification and support process should involve other agencies, if appropriate, such as health authorities and social work services.

The Bill recognises that parents need to be provided with information on identification and support, particularly since the Bill does acknowledge that it is not practical to have a uniform system throughout Scotland as LEAs work in different ways with different local arrangements and structures. LEAs are therefore required to publish local policies, arrangements and provision for young people with additional support needs and to describe the involvement of parents.

Other initiatives

In Scotland, many initiatives have been organised by dyslexia parent groups and some of these have been supported by the Scottish Executive. One such initiative was the SPIRE (Specific Information and Resources for Education) project that took place in the Highlands area of

Scotland. This was a Highlands-wide information service to parents to advise parents on issues relating to dyslexia, dyspraxia, autistic spectrum disorders and attention deficit hyperactivity disorder (ADHD). One of the features of this project was a mobile advice and information service to cater for the large geographical spread of the population in the Highlands area. Similar projects have taken place in other areas – for example, in Tayside, Parent to Parent Tayside produced CD-Roms which inform parents on the management of dyspraxia, dyslexia and autism.

Dyslexia Scotland have also implemented a number of exciting initiatives that benefit parents. This includes an 'E' forum where members can exchange ideas and ask questions on their home computers.

Additionally, in April 2004 an innovative resource, *Count Me In* (a staff development pack for teachers), was launched (Clark, 2004). This resource pack resulted from a government-funded initiative and although it is currently aimed at teachers an accompanying parent pack is envisaged.

Legislation lays only a framework – certainly an important one, but support groups and government initiatives such as those outlined above can make a significant, immediate and practical difference to parents, either through providing support, information and skills in advocacy, or through practical advice on literacy programmes and home literacy.

Republic of Ireland

A major initiative in the Republic of Ireland was the report of the Task Force on Dyslexia (July 2001). This far-reaching comprehensive government report was the result of deliberations of a government-appointed Task Force. The Task Force received 399 written submissions from individuals, educational institutions and organisations and 896 oral submissions were received from individuals by telephone. The report noted that parents in particular shared their views and frustrations with the Task Force. The report contains a summary of recommendations of particular interest to parents (p. xvii). The report said of parents:

> The vast majority of submissions came from you, the parents, who have first-hand experience of the learning difficulties arising from dyslexia

that are experienced by your children. We thank you for your contributions; we have read your comments carefully and we recognise the complex nature of your experiences and your needs.

As well as making 61 recommendations, the report provides an informative appendix showing indicators of learning differences, including those related to dyslexia for different age groups: age 3–5 years, 5–7 years, 7–12 years and over 12 years. Although the response to the report was positive, one of the concerns related to the implementation of the recommendations. It was important that the report was translated into practice, and there has been evidence that this is happening. In May 2002 it was announced that the Minister for Education and Science introduced new measures to ensure that some of the recommendations were carried out. These measures included the introduction of the first ever on-line training for teachers working with dyslexic pupils, the appointment of 10 new learning support trainers and substantially improved levels of teaching support for children with dyslexia by reducing the pupil–teacher ratio in special classes for dyslexia to 9 : 1.

In an address by the Minister for State at the 29th Annual Conference of the Irish Learning Support Teachers Association in Dublin, she indicated that the government aimed to half the number of pupils with serious literacy difficulties by 2006. She also applauded the joint North–South initiative which has resulted in the production of resources on dyslexia such as videos, CD-Roms and DVDs that will be distributed to schools.

Legislation in the USA

One of the most influential pieces of legislation that has a potential impact on parents and on 'dyslexia' is the No Child Left Behind Act (2001c). It is seen as a landmark in education reform in the USA and is designed to improve student achievement and change the culture of America's schools. President George W. Bush described this law as the cornerstone of his administration. It focuses on four main areas: accountability for results; an emphasis on doing what works based on scientific research; expanded parental options; and expanded local control and flexibility.

The No Child Left Behind Act targets resources for early childhood education so that all young children get the right start. Each State must measure every public school student's progress in reading and maths in each of grades 3–8 and at least once during grades 10–12. This education reform also requires that all States and school districts give parents easy-to-read, detailed report cards on schools and districts, telling them which ones are succeeding and why. Under the No Child Left Behind Act, such schools must use their federal funds to make needed improvements. In the event of a school's continued poor performance, parents have options to ensure that their children receive the high-quality education to which they are entitled. That might mean that children can transfer to higher-performing schools in the area or receive supplemental educational services in the community, such as tutoring, after-school programmes or remedial classes. The No Child Left Behind Act gives States and local education agencies more flexibility in the use of their federal education funding. There is also an emphasis on implementing educational programmes and practices that have been clearly demonstrated to be effective through rigorous scientific research.

Some of the key points of the No Child Left Behind Act that may help parents and children with dyslexia include the following: it gives schools more money; it holds schools accountable for results; it provides States and cities with more control and more flexibility to use resources where they are most needed; it focuses on teaching methods that have been proved to work; and it can allow parents to transfer their child to a better public school if the State says the school their child attends needs to improve.

The USA is also the main hub of the IDA mentioned earlier in this chapter. The IDA has branches in every State as well as affiliate branches in some other countries such as Brazil, the Czech Republic, Israel and the Philippines. The IDA is a very influential group; it is consulted in legislative reform and provides comprehensive advice and sources of support for parents.

New Zealand

Over the last decade education in New Zealand has gone through considerable changes. This particularly applies to Special Education, which is now seen as more uniform and less fragmented than previously.

There are a number of energetic parents' organisations in New Zealand such as the Specific Learning Difficulties Federation (SPELD) and the Learning and Behaviour Charitable Trust. SPELD is a non-profit-making organisation run by parents and teachers and was set up in 1971. It has three main objectives:

- **Advocacy** – that is, presenting submissions to government and organising publicity campaigns
- **Assessment and tutoring** – that is, providing assessments and tutoring services to schools and parents
- **Support** – that is, offering specialist services as well as training courses for parents and teachers.

SPELD also offers parents and teacher aide courses. The content of these include literacy, numeracy, how the brain works and practical ideas.

The Learning and Behaviour Charitable Trust was formed more recently. Its mission statement reflects

> the need to ensure young persons with dyslexia/attention difficulties receive an education based on equity and free from discrimination, to create more awareness of conditions relating to dyslexia and ADHD and to support families and young persons with learning and behavioural difficulties.

This organisation also runs events for parents and invites international speakers.

New Zealand is also fortunate in having a number of on-line education journals that are informative and accessible for parents and deal with issues relating to education, including dyslexia and other specific difficulties. The Ministry of Education also encourages parental participation and a number of well-established initiatives aimed directly at parents have been implemented such as the Parents as First Teachers (PAFT) programme, which was first implemented in 1991. Though this programme is not directly related to dyslexia, it does underline the principle of emphasising the role of parents in the education process. The programme was evaluated in 2003 and the evaluation report concluded that PAFT has much to offer families and society and that PAFT parents and families have an increased knowledge and understanding of children's learning (Farquhar, 2003).

Certainly in the parent association activity, SPELD has been the principal activist for many years and many SPELD tutors are widely recognised by parents and schools as having experience and expertise in the area of dyslexia. As indicated earlier this was recognised by the New Zealand government. It was interesting, therefore, to reflect on the responses of the parents who answered the questionnaire (see Gavin Reid's website) that helped to provide information for this book. Almost all mentioned having accessed a SPELD tutor at some point and many mentioned the SPELD workshops. Many also mentioned that helpful literature had been sent to them from the Learning and Behaviour Charitable Trust NZ (LBCTNZ).

The relatively recently created and extended role of the specialist Resource Teacher for Learning and Behaviour (RTLB) offers considerable hope for the future of children with dyslexia and therefore for parents. RTLBs undergo a comprehensive training course that includes significant elements on reading, dyslexia and specific difficulties.

Australia

SPELD also has an energetic organisation in Australia with a number of branches. For example, SPELD (South Australia) holds workshops for parents and gives advice on software and assistive technology. It also holds a major conference which attracts international speakers, and information evenings for parents. The conference held in Adelaide in July 2004 included a strand on 'working with parents'. Other organisations, such as Giorcelli Educational Consultancy Services (www.doctorg.org), provide high-quality educational services in all learning environments. Loretta Giorcelli, who is an established international figure, personally manages this organisation. Dr Giorcelli also runs successful workshops for parents, as well as for school professionals.

The Fun Track Learning Centre in Perth, West Australia, provides a range of exciting and motivational opportunities for children using their own unique learning styles, interests, strengths and needs. The children are encouraged to be active participants in the learning process through negotiated learning tasks, goal setting and reflections. The centre provides a supportive small group environment for children between the ages of 5 and 16 years old. The staff have experience in supporting children with a range of additional needs such as Dyslexia, ADD/ADHD, Central Auditory Processing Disorders, Visual Processing difficulties, Dysgraphia, Dyscalculia, Non-Verbal Learning Disorder and Semantic Pragmatic difficulties. Individual learning profiles and programmes are developed in consultation with the children, parents, any other involved professionals and through a range of standardised, diagnostic and cognitive profiling assessments. The centre is run by Mandy Appleyard, Principal Teacher and Educational Consultant. Email: mappleyard@funtrack.com.au Website: www.funtrack.com.au

Canada

Legislation in Canada, such as The School Act (British Columbia), is very much rooted in the practice of inclusion. This, while ultimately beneficial for most children, can bring a degree of confusion and anxiety for parents who may fear that their child's needs will not be met in large State schools.

The British Columbia Confederation of Parent Advisory Councils (BCCPAC) firmly believe that parents have a significant role to play in making things better for students in the public school system. They therefore organise Parent Advocacy Training and Advocacy Projects to enable parents to be more familiar with education programmes and be more effective partners in schools. The Learning Difficulties Association of British Columbia has been very effective in assisting parents and organising the above Parent Advocacy Training. It advocates the Orton–Gillingham approach, which is a multi-sensory structured and sequential approach used effectively in general education as well as special education, tutoring and home-school programmes.

A number of thriving organisations have emerged to support parents whose children need additional tuition. One such organisation in British Columbia is the organisation called Remedial Education for Adults and Children (REACH). This is an Orton–Gillingham Learning Center which offers one-to-one specialised teaching for children with dyslexia, summer camps and teacher and parent workshops. The REACH Learning Center was formed to assist individuals who are struggling with reading, writing and basic language skills. It is seen as complementary to the school curriculum. The important point is that if additional tuition is thought to be necessary, it is crucial that this is carried out by experienced and trained tutors, such as those involved in REACH.[1]

The Canadian Dyslexia Association, based in Ottawa,[2] uses trained instructors to run teaching sessions in the Simultaneous Multisensory Teaching (SMT) method. Similarly, the IDA British Columbia branch[3] has been active in producing information videos and in assisting families and individuals with a focus also on adults. One of the features of the education system in Canada is the notion of accountability. 'Accountability contracts' are a prominent part of school districts' accountability procedures. These contracts are based on information on student performance and reflect the results of foundation skills assessments, the achievement of special education students and the results of the parent, staff and student satisfaction surveys.

Individual education plans are also used in schools for children who have persistent difficulties in pre-academic areas, such as:

- recognition of letters and numbers in the early years
- persistent difficulties in the acquisition of reading, writing and/or arithmetic skills.

Individual plans may also be permitted to those who show a significant discrepancy between estimated learning potential and academic achievement, as measured by norm-referenced achievement instruments in grades 4–12.

Europe

The European Dyslexia Association (EDA) has long been established in Europe. It has risen to the challenge of the expanded Europe and embraced the newer European Community members into the main organisation. Indeed, it organised a major European conference in Budapest in 2003 to heighten the collaboration within the 'new' Europe, embracing the new member countries.

[1] www.reachlearningcenter.com
[2] www.dyslexiaassociation.ca
[3] www.interdys.org/jsp/bc.jsp

There are currently 29 countries represented in the EDA membership with a number of countries having more than one organisation as a member. The EDA also publishes a newsletter which is distributed to members and has an informative website (www.bedford.ac.uk/eda).

General comments

Although this chapter has focused, in the main, on a selection of individual countries, it should be noted that there are many other countries where legislation has made an impact on parents and/or children with dyslexia. There are many examples of parent support groups forming partnerships with others and engaging in many forms of lobbying, consultancy and support activities. For example, the Caribbean Dyslexia Association is developing a formal and approved dyslexia training course for teachers, and the Hong Kong Dyslexia Association has, for a number of years, organised comprehensive training courses for teachers and parents with international contributors.

Governments, too, have taken notice of the vigorous activities of parent associations and generally have attempted to collaborate with organisations through consulting with them and inviting representatives to contribute to investigations and developments in the field of SEN. In New Zealand, for example, the Education and Science committee reported on an enquiry into the teaching of reading, and positively noted the work of SPELD, indicating that the government should work closer with SPELD and that SPELD teachers should become more involved in mainstream schools.

Governments are, however, accountable to the electorate, and education departments are an integral part of that accountability. Results, and particularly results that can be measured, therefore appear to be a current preoccupation on the part of governments. There is a possibility that this can mitigate against children with dyslexia who may not receive the support they need because schools need to record and improve measurable performances. The progress of children with dyslexia cannot always be measured and may not fit into existing test paradigms.

Two other factors that have general application world-wide at present is the policy of inclusion and the notion of litigation. They may, in fact, be connected. Inclusion is a demanding concept for schools to implement successfully. It requires meeting the needs of diverse groups of children within the same educational setting. This, to be fully and successfully implemented, requires time, training and resources. Although there are many good examples of governments attempting to provide training and resources, in many countries and in many areas within countries, provision for dyslexia has still been described as patchy by local dyslexia associations. In fact, in one particular country, which has a very enlightened education policy and recognises the needs of children with dyslexia, the dyslexia association still received a vast amount of calls to their parental helpline. It could be, of course, that the best source of advice and support for parents are other parents.

It is always unfortunate when litigation is the result of any dispute or misunderstanding between two parties. There have been instances of litigation between parents and governments in relation to dyslexia in many countries. This usually arises because of either a failed diagnosis or a lack of appropriate intervention. These cases have often been test cases or landmark cases and have often resulted in more vigorous and constructive activity by governments to ensure that dyslexia is identified and that children with dyslexia are supported. In the UK in 1997, the well-known Phelps v. London Borough of Hillingdon case was decided in favour of Phelps because of a failure to diagnose dyslexia. The House of Lords confirmed this decision in July 2000 (David Ruebain).[4] There have also been other similar cases in the USA (Young & Browning, 2004) and Canada.[5]

The situation is improving considerably for children and adults with dyslexia and for parents. Much of this progress has been due to the actions and the determination of parents, individuals and particularly parent groups who have taken the initiative in many cases and resolutely lobbied government representatives.

There is certainly no shortage of rhetoric, of legislation promising equality, abolishing discrimination and minimising disability. There are also examples of this being translated into practice. However, there are still too many examples of the absence of appropriate support for, sometimes quite desperate, parents. In some cases, therefore, parents have no option but to pursue their rights through the law courts and

[4] www.ipsea.org.uk/phelps.htm
[5] www.poynerbaxter.com/Dyslexia.htm

there appears to be a plentiful supply of law firms willing to represent parents and adults in this way.

While this may be the only approach for some parents, it is never easy – any form of confrontation is a battle and one that can be, and usually is, stressful. This can often be unknowingly transmitted to the child. If law courts or tribunals are the only option remaining to parents, this approach needs to be handled sensitively and parent associations and trained counsellors and psychologists can provide helpful advice. The extent to which the child can be involved in the discussions depends on his or her age. The child, however, should be involved in some way and the parents need to find the most appropriate way of helping the child to understand what dyslexia means, and why his or her parents are following a particular course of action.

Summary

This chapter has provided a sample of insights into the practices, and particularly the role of parent groups, in different countries. The indication is that activity in teacher training and improvements in identification stemming from government initiatives are evident. Against this, however, there is also the situation of the 'brick wall' faced by many parents for whom the reality is, no identification, no recognition and no support (response to website questionnaire). This indicates that the recognition and identification of dyslexia are still not universally evident despite the significant scientific advances and information available through publications and on-line sources. It is not too surprising that legal avenues have been advanced by a number of individuals and parents. There is also a thriving independent sector comprising schools, groups and individuals, all of whom offer a complementary service to children and parents over and above, or instead of, what goes on in school. The work of these groups can be beneficial, the individuals are usually well trained, and if they liaise effectively with the child's school the collaboration can help to provide promising outcomes. This is beneficial for all parties and can be helpful for both school and parents.

Chapter 6

Beyond school

Questions and concerns of young people

After they leave school, the future of young people with dyslexia can be of some concern to parents and, of course, to the young person. Some of the questions and concerns that young people often harbour include:

- What type of work would I be able to do?
- Are there any professions/occupations I should avoid?
- Will I be supported in a college or university course?
- Will my employer consider my dyslexia and take it into account?
- What are the legal issues?
- Should I declare my dyslexia on my application forms?
- How can I help myself?

These are the types of questions and issues that young people with dyslexia, and their parents, are usually concerned about when the time comes for the young person to leave school. Some suggestions for dealing with these are shown below.

What type of work would I be able to do?

The short answer to that is simple – anything! If the young person has, for example, an interest in journalism, medicine, law or accountancy, then, with support, he or she can achieve that ambition. Certain occupations can be more challenging because of, and indeed depending on, the nature of the dyslexic difficulties, but no occupation should necessarily be ruled out.

Below there is a list of a number of popular professions and the type of challenges that can be faced by young people with dyslexia who may intend to enter these professions. Although this book is for parents it is still important that parents should be aware of the challenges the young person can face as often parents are the most readily available support for the young person, particularly when in a transitional stage from school to college or to work. The young person may have left previous contacts at school and not yet made any contacts with the information sources at college or the workplace.

Table 6.1 presents a chart of a number of potential professions that a person with dyslexia can enter. Every profession, no matter how dyslexia-friendly it might be, will contain some elements or tasks that can prove to be difficult for a dyslexic person. But the important points are, first, that the dyslexic person is not barred from any occupation because of his or her dyslexia, and, second, it is possible to work out accommodations, preferably with the support of the employer to support the dyslexic person in the workplace. This can be seen certainly in outline in Table 6.1.

Table 6.1 An A–Z of professions, challenges and accommodations for dyslexic people

Profession	Challenges	Accommodations
Armed forces	Entry qualifications, organisation, report-writing, reading fluently, remembering instructions	Lot of support available in the UK. Recognises the importance of supporting dyslexic people

Continues

Table 6.1 *Continues*

Profession	Challenges	Accommodations
Accountancy	Close and accurate number work, tables and statistics, memory work, examinations, detailed and accurate knowledge of tax legislation	Use of technology, working in teams, using dictaphone for reports
Art careers	Usually very well suited for dyslexic adults but can experience difficulty in examinations, and order and sequence of practical work	Use visual strategies, mind mapping to remember information
Building trades	Examinations, remembering quantities, ordering materials, figures, time management	Work in pairs, use calculator
Computer work	Usually very popular choice for dyslexic adults. Passing examinations, may include some maths, writing reports and letters, filing software and general administration work	Spend time to organise data and get some assistance with this if possible
Dentistry	Examinations, organisation, memory, record-keeping	Study skills support, memory strategies
Engineering	Usually a popular profession for dyslexic adults, mathematics, accuracy in figures and measurements, report-writing	Have formula prepared, work in teams
Fire services	Memory, report-writing, concise instructions	Usually team work is important

Profession	Challenges	Accommodations
Garage work	Report-writing, memory, visual skills, maybe maths and formulae	Customer relations important
Hairdressing	Ordering stock, remembering different lotions for different purposes, examinations	Develop customer relations and social skills
Insurance work	Maths, statistics may be necessary, accuracy with figures, report-writing	Use technology, calculators, software programs, dictaphone for letters
Journalism	Reading and writing at speed, summarising information, grammar and accuracy	Use dictaphone for interviews, use good word-processing package with advanced spell-check such as TextHelp©
Law	Entry qualifications may be high, a lot of reading, need to remember facts, need to be able to summarise information	Use secretarial support, use dictaphone, some good word-processing packages available for helping with summaries
Librarian	Accuracy in cataloguing, reading, ordering books sequencing, organisation	Take time to check and re-check. Ensure that you are familiar with the recording, shelving and filing system at the outset
Mechanic	Technical language, memory, maths and remembering diagrams	Mind mapping and other study techniques, take formulae into exams
Nurse	Exams, medical terminology, time-keeping, reading medicines, prescriptions	Working in teams, more time to check medicines, extra time for exams

Continues

Table 6.1 *Continues*

Profession	Challenges	Accommodations
Optician	Examinations, accuracy with figures, practical work, length of course	Take extra time to check figures
Police force	Entry qualifications, accuracy in reading, responding quickly	Use dictaphone to record notes
Restaurant work	Counting accurately, remembering orders, ordering materials	Write down everything including table number – try not to get flustered and develop good polite customer relations
Sales person	Remembering orders and product information	Use lightweight laptop computer to record information, use mind maps to remember product information
Teaching	Popular choice, need to be aware of your weaknesses, e.g. spelling, and try to compensate for these, planning lessons, organisation	Use strategies to ensure that you use your strengths. Plan well ahead so that you are not caught unawares by any situation
Vet	Long course, examinations, practical work, accuracy, memory	Use visual diagrams, work in teams, use the support assistance that is available
Youth worker	This is also a popular choice for adults with dyslexia. There will be examinations, memory work, and punctuality will be important	Work in teams, make sure that any legal and statutory implications of your work are explained to you rather than you having to read regulations

Profession	Challenges	Accommodations
Zoo worker	Remembering routine, ordering materials	Make a mind map of any duties such as time of feeding animals and type of food – ensure that the safety requirements are explained to you

It can be noted from this table that all professions, even those that are popular with dyslexic adults such as art and engineering, still provide challenges. Parents will therefore realise that dyslexia does not stop at school, but school can, in fact, prepare the young person for adult life. Parents need to ensure that their sons or daughters obtain appropriate career advice at an early age – before they decide on subject choices at secondary school. This is perhaps one of the most crucial aspects for a successful employment outcome for a young person with dyslexia.

Are there any professions/occupations I should avoid?

It can be noted from Table 6.1 that some occupations can be more challenging than others and may have more demanding entry qualifications for training courses, such as medicine and law. This should not prevent young people from applying for these courses as they will be supported if they receive a place. Furthermore, because there is now more support at school, more young people with dyslexia are achieving higher grades in school examinations and are gaining entry qualifications for courses such as law and medicine. This has a positive knock-on effect as tutors on these courses are increasingly gaining experience in dealing with dyslexic students, becoming more aware of what dyslexia is and more knowledgeable of the type of support required in both practical and theoretical work. There is still a long way to go before all staff in every university are comfortable and familiar with dyslexia, but that day will come and, of course, legislation in most countries supports the need to acknowledge and accommodate students with dyslexia.

Will I be supported in a college or university course?

The simple answer is 'Yes'! Most countries have legislation to support all students with a recognised disability, and dyslexia is recognised in terms of the legislation as a disability.

Most universities have guidance for students with dyslexia, or even those who suspect they might have dyslexia, but have not yet been diagnosed. This guidance can normally be accessed from the university web page. For example, Warwick University in the UK has information on what dyslexia is and what students can and should do. The university website indicates that

> Dyslexic students often find it difficult to give oral presentations. You may notice:
>
> ● increased anxiety if asked to present to a seminar group,
> ● difficulty reading from notes and a lack of fluency,
> ● a tendency to speak very fast.
>
> It is common to notice a marked discrepancy between seminar performance and written work. Students may also display short-term memory problems, making note-taking and copying from OHTs very difficult. Information may be taken down incorrectly.
>
> Students with dyslexia often work very hard, but their work may appear to show signs of carelessness. They find it difficult to proof-read and may not spot seemingly obvious mistakes.
>
> (Warwick University, UK – www2.warwick.ac.uk/
> services/tutors/disability/)

It is important, of course, to remember that the degree of severity of dyslexia can vary considerably. But all universities in the UK will have a disability coordinator and there is also an equivalent in the USA and in most other countries. The coordinator is a good point of contact for the student and can help with preparation and planning in advance of starting the course.

The legislation governing support for dyslexic students in the UK is the Special Educational Needs and Disability Act (2001) which forms Part IV of the Disability Discrimination Act.

According to the Act, discrimination can occur in two ways:

- By unjustifiably treating a disabled person less favourably for a reason relating to a person's disability.
- By failing to make a reasonable adjustment to avoid substantial disadvantage to the disabled person.

It is therefore unlawful for a responsible body to discriminate against a disabled person:

- in the arrangements it makes for admitting or enrolling students with a disability to their institution (this will occur from when the student has first made an enquiry about a course)
- in the terms on which it offers to admit or enrol a person
- by refusing or deliberately omitting to accept an application for admissions or enrolment
- in the provision of student services to those with a disability.

The services in this last point might include:

- teaching, including classes, lectures, seminars, practical sessions, field trips
- learning facilities such as classrooms, lecture theatres, laboratories
- learning equipment and materials such as laboratory equipment, computer facilities, class handouts and lecture notes
- arranging study abroad or work placements
- research degrees and research facilities
- informal/optional study skills sessions
- distance learning courses and support
- libraries, learning centres, information centres and their resources
- careers advice and training.

One of the key points in this legislation is the notion of 'reasonable adjustment'. This means that institutions must take reasonable steps to ensure that a disabled student is not placed at a substantial disadvantage in comparison with someone who is not disabled.

An important point is that the institution's responsibility to make reasonable adjustment is an anticipatory duty, which means that they have to pre-plan to ensure that the institution is equipped to deal with the range of needs that can be required by disabled students. One of the implications of this is, in fact, a question that parents and young people often ask: Should dyslexia be disclosed in the application form? The answer to that is 'Yes' because if it is not disclosed the institution will have no statutory obligation to provide additional support for the student. If it is disclosed, then the institution will need to acknowledge this in terms of the legislation.

However, in the USA, Young and Browning (2004) provide a different perspective and show that some groups of young dyslexic adults may still be disadvantaged. They suggest that studies indicate that (identified) persons with learning disabilities/dyslexia in employment and education tend to show only marginal differences in success compared to those with other disabilities. Furthermore, they argue that these employment studies, and other studies of persons with learning disabilities/dyslexia, tend to focus mainly on white males who had been identified, had received special educational services and had graduated from high school. The NICHD research, according to Young and Browning, strongly indicates that two-thirds of those with learning disabilities/dyslexia who had not been identified by the school systems within the USA and the UK tended to be poor, if not very poor, disproportionately female and minority, and as they had not been identified they had not received services and, more often than not, had not graduated from high school.

There is clearly a role here for careers and other school personnel to ensure that the route is open and opportunities are available for all young adults who may be in this position. Parents, therefore, have a role to play here, and if they are unable, for whatever reason, to articulate their demands, then support groups need to take on that role. It is important, therefore, that parents do make contact with dyslexia support groups if they suspect their young son or daughter may be dyslexic, but has not been identified at school.

Glen Young (personal communication) coined the phrase 'information deficit disorder' to describe those students (and adults) with learning disabilities/dyslexia, who not only fall behind in school owing to poor reading skills, but also fail to gain knowledge in any area because the information is usually provided in written form. Therefore, while struggling to gain reading skills, the student is also falling further behind in developing a knowledge base that would allow him or her to compete.

Young and Browning maintain that self-advocacy skills are among the most critical skills necessary for the adult in systems of all kinds, whether education, training, employment or financial assistance. These skills, however, need to be developed at school. They suggest that young people with dyslexia;

- need to understand the laws and regulations concerning reasonable accommodations, and their right to have these accommodations in the workplace and in higher education;
- need to know how to ask for what they want and to use accommodations as part of the general adult education process;
- need to have the ability and the opportunity to discuss these issues, as this can be the key to success in the transition through various phases of the learning experience in college and in the workplace.

Young and Browning support the notion of using the disability model as they suggest that the use of this model helps to 'shift the power relationships' between the person with learning disabilities/dyslexia and programmes and work. For example, if an individual comes into the workplace and says, 'I learn differently,' the employer is not legally required to provide any kind of accommodation. On the other hand, the individual who says 'I have a disability' creates a situation in which the employer is required to provide reasonable accommodations that would allow the employee with a disability to perform his or her job and compete on a level playing field.

David McLoughlin, however, from the Adult Dyslexia and Skills Development Centre in London, suggests that if dyslexic people are to be fully *included* in society the emphasis should be on empowerment or enablement rather than on a model of disability that perceives the 'dyslexic as a victim'(McLoughlin, 2004). He suggests that empowerment comes from:

- Self-understanding. Dyslexia is often referred to as a 'hidden disability'. Dyslexic people therefore have to advocate for themselves, and can only do so if they have a good understanding of the nature of their difficulty, how it affects them and what they need to do to improve their performance.

● Understanding by others, particularly employers. If dyslexic people have to deal with managers and colleagues whose understanding of the nature of dyslexia is limited, it is likely that the dyslexic person will be excluded, rather than included.

McLoughlin (2004) goes on to suggest that the persistence of dyslexia in the adult years raises important issues about the definition of dyslexia, with consequent implications for practice. To take advantage of the provisions of the Disability Discrimination Act (1995), for example, individuals do not have to establish that they are dyslexic but that their difficulties constitute a disability that has significant adverse day-to-day effects. A narrow literacy-based view of dyslexia will not protect dyslexic people from discrimination, nor will it oblige employers to make adjustments that will 'level the playing field'.

It is important to recognise that dyslexia is contextual (Reid, 2003). That means that the work context is important and the degree and the extent to which dyslexia will affect the individual will depend on the actual task demands and the work environment.

Will my employer consider my dyslexia and take it into account?

This can be a bit more tricky, although in terms of equity legislation, employers in most countries will have to take dyslexia into account. There are, of course, many loopholes, but employers do need to ensure that they have made appropriate accommodations to support the dyslexic person. Much, of course, depends on the understanding of the employer and it can be difficult for the dyslexic young person if the employer is not sympathetic to dyslexia. It is always best to avoid confrontation and recourse to the law, but, of course, that is always an option.

It does not really require too much effort for the employer to take dyslexia into account. It may mean teaming people together so that the dyslexic person is with someone who can give support (and similarly the dyslexic person can support others who are not dyslexic!), providing some software that can help with spelling, and organising and summarising information. Providing more time for some kind of tasks – for example, those that require a substantial amount of reading and writing – and perhaps ensuring that the dyslexic person is employed in an area of work that will highlight his or her strengths rather than his or her difficulties, are some examples of what can be done.

What are the legal issues?

In most countries the law is currently in favour of young people with dyslexia. The legislation in the UK and the USA and in other countries was described in Chapter 5. The key point, however, relates to identification and disclosure. Before the individual has any recourse to the law, he or she must be professionally assessed and diagnosed. Furthermore, it is necessary to share this information with employers or college and university officials to ensure that an adequate opportunity has been provided to implement appropriate support.

Should I declare my dyslexia on my application forms?

In view of the above, the correct answer to that question is 'Yes', but, of course, in practice a 'Yes' may not be best in the short term. But I strongly suggest that dyslexic people should always declare their dyslexia on an application form. Legally this should not discriminate against them and it informs the prospective employer at the outset, so that if a dyslexic person is employed, the employer will be made aware of the accommodations that will have to be made.

In some professions the applicant may think that dyslexia will not be an issue because of the nature of the work and so may be inclined not to declare it to an employer. This needs careful thought as job descriptions can change with or without promotion to another post. It is better, therefore, to let the employer know at the outset so that if a promoted post or change of duties occurs, the employer will be aware of the need to make appropriate accommodations.

McLoughlin, however, argues that demonstrating that there are difficulties in carrying out normal day-to-day activities can still be difficult. Dyslexia is not well understood as an information-processing difficulty and employers, as well as lawyers, are likely to focus mainly on literacy skills. Literate dyslexics are, he claims, in a difficult position.

He suggests that those supporting dyslexic people need to focus on the extent of the information processing and the legislation does specifically refer to the person's ability to remember, to organise his or her thoughts, to plan a course of action and execute it, or to take in new knowledge. Someone who has good academic qualifications and advanced literacy skills, but needs to get to work much earlier than everyone else and leave later in order to complete all the tasks that would be required in a normal day, is being affected on a day-to-day basis, and it is important that this situation is conveyed to employers. Parents and careers personnel can have an important role to play, particularly in helping the dyslexic individual to develop the self-advocacy skills mentioned below.

How can I help myself?

This is an important question as, at the end of the day, it is really up to the individual how he or she deals with dyslexia. Self-help is usually the best type of help as the individual is in complete control. Others can tell the dyslexic young person what might be best, or how to deal with a certain challenging situation at work, but each dyslexic person is different, each is an individual and therefore the most effective way to deal with any challenging situation is on an individual basis. It can also be best if the young person with dyslexia takes the lead.

This, of course, may be easier said than done for some young people. Parents can help by discussing with the young person how they tackle situations and how they may improve on their method of tackling something. It could be that after discussing it with a parent or family member they realise that all they need to do is to improve on their filing system, diary-keeping or prioritising some areas of work or changing the sequence of tasks. A parent can provide a listening ear and pass on supportive and non-threatening advice. But it is the individual who must act on it.

Career advice

Reid and Kirk (2001) show how many people with dyslexia have succeeded in a variety of occupations. McLoughlin (2004), who indicates
that being dyslexic is not necessarily a barrier to occupational success,
supports this. He says

> There are too many dyslexic people in all occupations to refute this,
> but some occupations are more dyslexia-friendly than others, tapping
> the dyslexic person's strengths rather than their weaknesses. There are
> undoubtedly dyslexic people who are in the wrong job, that is, they are
> in a situation where the demands on tasks they find difficult outweigh
> those on their competencies and strengths. Career guidance/counselling
> geared towards the needs of dyslexic people is arguably one of the most
> important, but under-resourced professional activities
>
> (McLoughlin, 2004, p. 180)

Without doubt, ongoing career advice is important. This will allow the
young person to have several choices and if one does not work out he
or she will be able to discuss this with the careers person. Key points
for career advice would be: before subject choice in secondary school;
before applying to college or university; when applying for a job; and
after having been in employment for a period of time to discuss how
the dyslexic person may advance in that career or an alternative one.
Some questions a parent/young person may want to know from a careers
adviser are noted below.

Questions to a careers adviser

Questions to a careers adviser can include the following areas and
issues:

- What are the entry qualifications for the course?
- What is the availability of places in training courses?
- What is the length of training?
- What amount of written skills is needed for the occupation, or course
  of training?
- What is the competition for recruitment?

- What are the career prospects?
- Would I need to travel a long distance to work?
- Are there time pressures associated with the work?
- Will there be any work that demands accuracy with figures?

When applying for a job the young person will also need to consider these points. These are discussed below.

Transition to work

There are a number of factors that need to be considered when applying for, and commencing, employment. These are the interview, the preparation for employment, and settling into new employment. Although at this stage young people tend to be independent of their parents, that is not always the case and parents can provide advice and certainly be on hand to give advice if the young person asks for it. Parents at this stage need to tread a balance between being on hand to give advice, if necessary, and allowing the young person to gradually develop independence and take responsibility for his or her decisions. In many ways this is what parenting is all about, but young people with dyslexia can have additional sensitivity related to their dyslexia and this can be a slightly more vulnerable phase for young people.

The interview and the job

Young people need advice and support before a job or college interview. Again parents may be a good source of this advice. There is some general advice that parents can provide, or indeed the young person can consider. This includes:

Preparation for the interview

- Try to ensure that you know exactly where the interview is being held. It may be an idea to check out the area and the venue of the interview the day before so that you will know exactly where to go. This will be one less thing for you to think about and will make it easier to concentrate only on the interview.

- Ensure that you arrive in good time – not too early, but certainly not at the last minute. It is important to be relaxed before an interview and rushing at the last minute will create panic, not relaxation.
- Try to have some idea of how long the interview will last. This will help you to pace your answers and you will have an idea of how much time is left, which can help you to work out when to ask any questions you wish to ask.
- Try to find out who will be interviewing you and how many people will be present. This may avoid the unexpected.
- Take advice on how to dress for an interview.
- Rehearse an answer in your mind to a possible question you may be asked about your dyslexia, and how it has affected you. You may wish to describe how you have coped with it and the strengths you have used to overcome any difficulties.

Preparation for employment

- It may be a good idea to have a pre-meeting with your employer to satisfy yourself that your dyslexia will not be a problem in the type of work you will be doing.
- If your employer is not aware of what dyslexia is, this might be a good time to explain it.
- Try to work out the best route you can take to work so that you will not be late on the first day.
- The best form of preparation for any job of work is to rest and be relaxed before you start. Starting a new job can be quite exhausting, and as you will need to be in peak condition it is best to rest beforehand.

Settling into new employment

It can often take a young person a little time to settle into a new occupation. The challenges of new employment are different for each person and also depend on the type of work that has to be carried out. Once you know exactly what your work duties are, you may want to try to anticipate the kind of duties that may cause you some worry. Some general workplace difficulties are listed below:

- filing documents/retrieving files
- following detailed instructions
- remembering routines
- writing letters and memos
- writing reports
- summarising and presenting ideas in presentations
- getting the times and places of meetings wrong
- missing appointments.

These difficulties can be managed by:

- reading words slowly and carefully
- breaking sentences down into short phrases
- skimming text to get an overall picture before reading for detail
- using colour-coding for different pieces of information
- labelling box files and filing trays
- making a checklist of tasks to be completed, and you may have to work one step at a time.

If I were to identify any one aspect that is crucial to the above it would be communication. Parents in their supportive role can ensure that the person with dyslexia has the confidence and the opportunity to communicate with employers and is able to ask the right questions.

Summary

This chapter will be of benefit to the young person with dyslexia who has left, or is about to leave, school. Although, quite rightly, the young person is gaining in independence and is less reliant on his or her parents for direction, parents' views are still often sought. The objective of this chapter, therefore, is to help the parents by providing some guidance that may help them to advise their son or daughter. This is no easy matter as dyslexia can assume different forms. I have indicated in this chapter that dyslexia can be described as contextual. This means that it can have a varying impact, depending on the situation, the nature of the work, or indeed the type of course of study that is to be completed.

This chapter answers some fundamental questions that can be of interest to parents, teachers or careers personnel and by teenagers with dyslexia. To recap, these questions are:

- What type of work would I be able to do?
- Are there any professions/occupations I should avoid?
- Will I be supported in a college or university course?
- Will my employer consider my dyslexia and take it into account?
- What are the legal issues?
- Should I declare my dyslexia on my application forms?
- How can I help myself?

By answering these questions it is hoped that this chapter has provided some advice and guidance to parents. Parents can be in a difficult position as they want to help but at the same time need to allow the young person a degree of independence. In treading this delicate balance it is best if parents at least have some knowledge, understanding and even some facts at their fingertips. This will enable parents to provide the type of advice and, more importantly, the support the young person may really need.

Chapter 7

Parents' and children's voices

The aim of this chapter is to highlight some of the experiences and views of parents of children with dyslexia. The research for this chapter was obtained from questionnaires and interviews with parents (and children) in different countries of the world. It was interesting to note how parents' experiences differed – even among those parents living in the same areas.

One of the points to emerge from the research evidence gathered for this book is that, however careful and sensitive the education authority/ system might be in developing procedures for identifying and dealing with dyslexia, there will still be a number of parents whose needs are simply not met. This situation can arise for a number of reasons, including misunderstandings and communication difficulties between the school and parents. Often parents' needs are not met because of a reluctance on the part of the school system to accept the common understanding of dyslexia and to recognise that children with dyslexia do require a different form of intervention. The difficulties experienced by some parents are noted in some of the examples in this chapter. These relate to the difficulties parents can experience in accessing the resources and provision for their child, but the examples also highlight how difficulties can be overcome. It is heartening to note some of the successes experienced by parents.

Parents' anxieties

Parents can experience anxieties throughout the process of identification. They may have to attend formal meetings that they normally would not attend and may have to assert their views when it is not in their nature to be assertive. It is important that professionals recognise this and appreciate that it is their duty to ensure that parental anxieties are kept to a minimum. Parents will find discussing their concerns with other parents very helpful. Those who responded to the questionnaire for this book highlighted this very strongly.

As part of the research for this book I undertook a number of interviews with parents as well as placing a parent questionnaire on my web home page. Parents were requested to complete the questionnaire online and all respondents provided address details in order that follow-up information could be obtained. The following questions were presented:

- What are the factors that made it difficult for you as a parent of a child with dyslexia?
- From whom did you get your support?
- What strategies did you, as a parent, use to help to support your son or daughter with dyslexia ?

This chapter will provide some insights into these questions and highlight some of the key issues to emerge from the responses. The chapter will also answer some of the additional questions and issues that have been raised by parents.

Parents' responses

Factors that make it difficult for parents

This section provides details of the responses from some of the parents and this is followed by some of the general observations from all the responses gathered.

One parent's responses

One of the parents who responded found that the main challenges in parenting a child with dyslexia included:

- helping to maintain the child's self-esteem
- helping the child start new work when he or she had not consolidated previous work
- protecting the dignity of the child when dealing with professionals/ therapists
- personal organisation of the child
- peer insensitivity
- misconceptions of dyslexia.

These responses are quite interesting because they touch on some of the key areas, particularly the emotional aspect of dyslexia. They also touch on the misunderstandings and misconceptions that many can have of dyslexia.

Emotional aspects

It can be too easy to ignore the emotional aspects of dyslexia. Often the child's main difficulty will relate more directly to learning and to literacy, and this can be the main area of concern. If a child, however, is failing in literacy and finds school work challenging, then it is likely that he or she will suffer emotionally. It is important that this is addressed and preferably prevented.

The parent who provided the above responses suggested that helping to maintain the child's self-esteem, dealing with peer insensitivity and helping to preserve the child's dignity when dealing with professionals are crucial. I have selected these responses because they seem to accurately pinpoint the factors that have the potential to undermine a child's self-esteem.

Children can be very sensitive, particularly if they feel they are, in any way, different from others. Children with dyslexia usually have to visit psychologists and other specialists. For some children this can indicate that they are different and they may feel stigmatised as a consequence of this. Even young adults at college and university can experience these feelings. Assessments and support for students with dyslexia are very often carried out at the 'disability office' within the college or university and many do not want, or in fact need, the 'disability label' and may be reluctant to enter an office which is clearly labelled – 'disability office'.

This highlights the importance of full, frank and informative feedback following an assessment with the child or young adult, as well as with the parents. In fact, this initial feedback is as important as the eventual follow-up and intervention.

There are a number of ways of helping to maintain and boost children's self-esteem, but one of the most obvious and most effective ways is to ensure that they achieve some success and genuine praise. In order for praise to be effective the child has to be convinced that the praise is worthy of his or her achievements. When children feel that they have failed, it is difficult to reverse these feelings and often they need to change their perceptions of themselves. This can be a lengthy process and ongoing support, praise and sensitive handling are necessary.

The parent whose comments are discussed above suggested that she had found the following very useful for her child:

- training in positive thinking
- paired reading
- mind mapping, including software mapping
- memory games
- learning styles
- opportunity for the child to use to use verbal ability and to benefit from discussion
- focusing on areas of success.

This parent also provided additional information and suggested that

Self-esteem is a huge issue and one that is not helped by dyslexia being seen as a deficit! The continued emphasis on academic achievement and the issues of labelling are problematic for me. A major difficulty with the teaching profession is attitudinal – a lack of knowledge on dyslexia is apparent, although I have found there are also some exceptional teachers, but it is always difficult for a parent to know what advice to take. By the time they are in a position to decide it can be too late, or less effective than it could have been.

The balance between home and school is a key issue and although I have had little advice on this I have still had to argue a case for the need for school to understand the fatigue element in a long day. I feel like my child is a square peg in a round hole.

Within the questionnaire, parents were invited to make additional comments. Some of the additional comments made by parents make interesting reading and clearly indicate not only the frustrations often experienced by parents, but the energies they display to ensure that their child's needs are acknowledged within the education system.

One parent from the north of England said:

> We lived with the effects of our son's dyslexia ... there was a failure to recognise that he had a learning difficulty at school and this had a very negative effect as the school labelled him as 'behavioural' but also said he was polite and not the typical 'thug'. No teacher ever mentioned he had learning problems at school – when he was tested at almost 16 years of age his auditory memory was at a six-year-old level.

Another parent, from the south of England, suggested that getting the school to recognise the problem and obtaining a firm diagnosis of dyslexia was a difficulty, as well as trying to find out where to get advice and help. This parent also suggested that the local Dyslexic Association was, for her, an excellent first port of call and offered a wealth of information.

Legislation was reported in a very positive way in Chapter 5, which gives information about the 'Parent Partnership Scheme' (PPS) in England and Wales – an initiative that has resulted from legislation.

The above parent, however, in responding to the questionnaire, suggested that the PPS was, at least for her:

> useless and unable to help me find support for my son within the educational process, it made me ask 'Whose side they are on?'

This parent, however, provided some very positive advice, such as

> 'Remember to take time out.' 'Have fun as a family.' 'Home is a safe place, no criticism, try not to push, push, push. Encourage your child to peruse the things he/she is good at. Keep self-esteem high. Set up good working relationship with the school teacher.' 'Keep trying, there is help available, just keep chipping away.'

Another parent, from the East Anglia area of England, said that the PPS was a great source of help. This may have been because this parent said that she suffered from a lack of understanding of the education system and found this very frustrating. Another parent also mentioned frustration with the education system and said:

> We feel frustrated by the education system – we know there is no quick fix but constantly feel we are just being pacified by the school management. We know as soon as our son moves to the high school he will no longer be a problem for the primary school's statistics.

It is interesting to note, however, that a parent from a neighbouring education authority to the previous one suggested that

> I am very aware that I have been very fortunate that the education services in our education authority have provided teachers with up to date training in dyslexia and this has greatly benefited me and my dyslexic children. Having a teacher who is very aware of dyslexia and understanding is incredibly supportive.

One parent from Ohio in the USA, who decided to home-school her dyslexic son, listed the struggles that had to be endured. These included being

> accused of not understanding him, accused of showing favouritism between him and his other siblings, teaching him to read, keeping his attention and making him want to learn, finding the right resource and finding people who are supportive to me.

The comments produced here may well be familiar to many readers. In fact, I asked a colleague who is a parent of an adult dyslexic daughter – who is now a very successful professional – of her lasting recollections as a parent of a daughter with dyslexia. Although her daughter had left school well over 10 years earlier, my colleague without too much hesitation suggested two key factors. One factor was not having her 'able and gifted' attributes recognised by the school. She was essentially treated as a slow learner. Secondly, the emotional damage, and, indeed, the lasting emotional damage, that can result even when the outcome is favourable and the person emerges as a skilled, successful, mature adult in a demanding profession. It is reasonable to suggest that most parents are aware of the emotional factors that can accompany dyslexia. But they may not be aware of the potential endurance of these factors even when life events become favourable for that person.

This fear of some possible long-lasting emotional damage is perhaps the catalyst that spurs parents to search, often desperately, for some 'cure' for dyslexia. One set of parents, from New Zealand, who responded to the questionnaire, commented on the financial outlay involved in helping to find the right intervention for their child. Eventually they settled on home-schooling. But they did comment on the various interventions and additional and costly range of supports they had used, and paid for, and remarked that 'they did not help at all'. Spending money and engaging in a glossy or promising treatment, it seems, is not always the best recourse.

Key issues

Some of the key issues to emerge from the above and from some of the other responses are mentioned below.

1. Frustration

Parents can experience frustration with the education system. This may not necessarily be a problem with the system, but a problem stemming from a breakdown in communication and different priorities and agendas.

Without question, all schools and all teachers want to do their best for all children. Schools, however, have to meet the needs of individuals as well as the common needs of all learners. Teachers have also to meet the demands placed on them by the management and the education system. These demands are usually set by politicians and are often based on principles relating to accountability and results. These principles can present a difficulty in relation to dyslexia because progress made by children with dyslexia may not always be easily measured, and certainly not by conventional means. For example, for some children with dyslexia merely attending school can be a measure of success, but schools may not record this as progress and would rather focus on progress on attainments such as reading, spelling and writing. This is perfectly reasonable but children with dyslexia may not make significant progress in this area, at least in the short term, which can lead to some frustration on the part of parents and highlight very clearly the different agendas that can be seen between home and school. This underlines the importance of effective and shared communication.

2. Trust

Different perspectives can lead to a degree of mistrust. This is obviously a negative emotion and one that can seriously damage the relationship between home and school. It can sometimes be difficult for parents to place their trust in a system that may not even seem to recognise dyslexia, but this is exactly what they have to do! Some parents who responded to the questionnaire in fact suggested that they are a source of information on dyslexia for the school. It is a question of balance – not only of placing some trust in the education system, but also of ensuring that you are aware of exactly what is going on in school regarding your child's education. There may be differences of opinions between home and school, but these should not break down any trust between the two. Parents are permitted to question and to seek explanations from school on how their child is being educated, but it is best to use this right in a constructive manner.

3. Balance

Parents often ask how they balance the stress their child can experience in school work with life at home. This can be a difficult point as often the stress that can be experienced at school can spill over into home life, especially since potential stresses, such as homework, can take up an undue amount of time at home. One parent indicated very strongly in the questionnaire that work at home should be fun. This may be difficult to achieve without making light of the work that the child has to do, but what this parent meant was that the family should try to provide a fun environment that will be free from stress. She suggested that the family should try to provide fun-type activities or games that can provide learning strategies for the child. This can be the use of mnemonics or even board games, both of which can be useful for developing memory skills. One parent from south-west Scotland who responded to the questionnaire suggested that, for her, games were extremely important in ensuring that her son did not take the stress at school into the home. She suggested the following:

> 'Kitchen cupboards' is a favourite. You have to identify all the products in the kitchen, play around with the products using part of the name, adding it on to part of another products name. For example, we may take flour, marmalade, milk, washing powder and work our way through the different combinations of sounds from each of the products. From this we make up silly products like 'marwashder'. My son remembers the sounds and combinations much more easily when I relate it to some fun activity.

4. Understanding

Another of the issues relates to understanding. Many parents indicated that schools, or some teachers in schools, did not have much knowledge of dyslexia. This clearly varies from country to country and, indeed, within countries from area to area. Additionally, the level of knowledge of dyslexia within a school will be different. Parents need to realise this and may have to take it upon themselves to inform the school of some of the current interventions and thinking in dyslexia. At the same time, however, there does appear to be a considerable thrust in schools, and within education authorities, to increase teacher training and whole school awareness of dyslexia (Reid, 2001, 2003).

Having spoken on dyslexia to parent associations in many different countries, this is becoming very apparent and, almost without exception, a scheduled and advertised talk to a parent association will find many teachers in the audience. It is important that parents understand what dyslexia is and this should be explained to them as soon as their child is assessed, and it is equally important that teachers also know the different aspects relating to dyslexia.

5. Emotions

As indicated above, emotional factors are an important consideration for parents and can be a real concern to children and adults with dyslexia. Indeed many parents, due to the anxieties they experience and the frustrations they can encounter, can become emotionally affected. As a parent of a young man with autism, I know only too well of the long-lasting emotional impact of supporting and living through crisis and trauma. Parents do become affected if they do not seek out the best form of support (which is usually other parents), and if they continually see their child's education in terms of a 'struggle'. One parent remarked at the end of the questionnaire: 'I am very cynical.' This is unfortunate, and although this type of emotion can be destructive, it can also be appreciated why, in some situations, parents feel like this.

An interesting university study was conducted by Terras and colleagues (2004) jointly with the Dyslexia Institute, Scotland, called: '"I feel very, very small": Reflections on living with dyslexia'. The study was conducted on six adults with dyslexia and concluded that dyslexia was experienced by the group as having a negative impact on:

- self-esteem
- social/emotional well-being
- relationships
- daily life, education and choice of careers.

Low self-esteem is often accompanied by negative emotions. In the above study one respondent said: 'If you are comfortable in the environment you are in, you get on well, but if you feel threatened in any way, you will draw into yourself.' This highlights a crucial point about the environment. Children, and adults, will learn more effectively if they feel comfortable in the school. They must feel they belong there and that they are being treated fairly. One adult reflected, 'If you are dyslexic, you are bullied all the time,' and another said, 'I just disappeared into a corner somewhere and just hoped the teacher wouldn't get me.'

Yet it should not be all doom and gloom. Many with dyslexia have succeeded to a high level and have become confident and well-adjusted adults. This, of course, is the hope of every parent of a child with dyslexia and, to be fair, the quest of every teacher. There are, however, many influences along the way that can prevent this from happening. Yet there is more support available in dyslexia than ever before and more scientific advances that allow parents and teachers to understand the causes and characteristics of dyslexia.

Questions parents ask

There are many different aspects to dyslexia and there are many questions and anxieties that parents may harbour. Parents may get answers to these questions from schools, but the school may not have answers to all the questions that trouble parents. If this is the case, parents should have an opportunity to ask other parents these questions at parent association meetings, or when they have an invited guest speaker. Some of the questions I was asked at a recent talk to parents included the following:

- How can parents help at home with the dyslexic child's organisational difficulties?
- Dyslexic children seem to be more susceptible to infections. Have you found this to be the case?
- What are your views on children being given fish oil supplements?
- What are your views on exercise programmes such as Dyslexia, Dyspraxia and Attention Treatment (DDAT) for dyslexic children? Are you cautious or confident?
- When do you decide to give up on reading with a severely dyslexic child? How much should you push him or her? At what stage do you decide to go for a scribe and reader to allow the child to progress through the curriculum?
- Will a child who is diagnosed with dyslexia grow out of it?
- How can you tell the difference between a poor speller and a dyslexic child?
- If my child is diagnosed with dyslexia, should I give up on him or her entering tertiary education?
- If my child requires a scribe and reader for examinations, how will the child cope with a job when he or she leaves education?

I have chosen to use these particular questions in this book and in this chapter because they are general questions that have come from parents. Quite often at parent meetings many of the questions relate to specific instances and incidents at the child's school – and it is difficult to answer such questions without knowledge of the actual situation in the classroom. The questions selected here, however, can be answered fairly informatively without too much knowledge of the child's specific educational context. Responses to these questions are shown below.

- **How can parents help at home with the dyslexic child's organisational difficulties?**

Perhaps the best way to answer this question is to suggest that children with dyslexia do not have organisational difficulties, but, in fact, have organisational differences. Certainly they may have difficulty in time-tabling and remembering appointments and homework, but they do have the ability to organise themselves. It must, however, be done their way and they must assume responsibility for this. A parent can certainly help by structuring and even suggesting ways of remembering information. It is best and most effective, however, if the child, supported by the parents, can develop his or her own method of organisation.

It is important not to equate tidiness with being organised. The essential aspect of being organised is that information and items can be remembered and retrieved when required. This may seem easier to do if everything is in place and the child has a tidy desk, bag or bookshelf, but quite often children with dyslexia remember and organise themselves visually and this can be quite different from the methods used by their parents. Children with dyslexia may give the impression of being disorganised when, in fact, functionally they **are** organised. The simple answer to this question is to be supportive and understanding, and although parents can also try to suggest various ways of organising and remembering information, they should insist that children must decide what is best for themselves.

- **Dyslexic children seem to be more susceptible to infections. Have you found this to be the case?**

I am not aware of any evidence to support this except to suggest that if any child is under stress – whether obvious stress or hidden stress – the person will be more susceptible to many ailments, including infections. I would always emphasise a healthy diet with a range of fruit and vegetables and cutting down, or cutting out, sugar and food or drink additives. This will make the child more alert and better able to cope with the stressful demands of a school curriculum that is usually dominated by literacy.

There is some evidence from genetics that some of the genes that can relate to dyslexia are also the same genes that can be implicated with the autoimmune system (Snowling, 2000). This can, therefore, emphasise the need to ensure a healthy diet and, if necessary, the use of vitamin supplements.

- *What are your views on children being given fish oil supplements?*
- *What are your views on exercise programmes such as Dyslexia, Dyspraxia and Attention Treatment (DDAT) for dyslexic children? Are you cautious or confident?*

These two questions are dealt with in Chapter 8 of this book on alternative interventions. In brief, however, many children will benefit from taking fish oil supplements. The research of Alex Richardson and colleagues (Richardson & Puri, 2000; Richardson, 2001) has been very influential and has highlighted the importance of this in relation to dyslexia and other specific learning difficulties, such as dyspraxia and attention disorders.

In answer to the question on programmes such as DDAT, I would suggest that I am both cautious and confident. Every new innovation and treatment needs to be dealt with cautiously, but everyone needs to have confidence in the research and evaluations of these innovations. It is not possible to have confidence in a treatment until properly controlled evaluations have been carried out. This will also be dealt with in the next chapter.

- *When do you decide to give up on reading with a severely dyslexic child? How much should you push him or her? At what stage do you decide to go for a scribe and reader to allow the child to progress through the curriculum?*

The direct answer to the first part of this question is that you never give up. The best course of action is to try to ensure that the child has opportunities to read all the way through school and as an adult. As they go through school, children with dyslexia will improve in reading. Some children may always lag well behind their chronological age in reading but they will increasingly obtain more meaning from print and, of course, this needs to be encouraged. It is interesting to note that with a reading age of around 11 years, one will be able to read most of the popular newspapers.

At the same time you do not want to 'push' the child and increase the stress he or she can associate with reading. The key is to find ways of making reading more interesting and accessible. This can be done by using different forms of books and text. For example, Barrington Stoke have a set of readers specifically written for reluctant readers. These readers have a high interest level and the vocabulary will be at a lower level than the interest level of the book. This makes the child more motivated to read the book. If the reading material is of interest to the child, then he or she will want to persevere. Children who have difficulty in reading fluently, however, can use speech-related software that can read the book to them or use taped books. Additionally, it should be recognised that to get meaning from print, one does not need to read every word and to have 100% reading accuracy. Competent readers rarely read every word when reading silently, yet can gain full meaning from the text. The key is to provide the child with enriched language experience so that he or she can develop concepts and be able to read for context and meaning more easily. Watching a video of the book first can provide the child with the story line, and this can help him or her use context and guess the words that are difficult to read or at least obtain sufficient meaning from the words that are easier to read.

In answer to the last part of the question – at what stage do you decide to go for a scribe and reader to allow the child to progress through the curriculum? – you can usually tell fairly early on in the child's education if he or she will need some additional support with reading in particular. Certainly by the time of transfer to secondary school or during middle school, some kind of decision should be made. This may appear quite early to some but the key point is that if the student is to require a reader or scribe, then he or she needs practice at using this facility. One of the important points in relation to this are the views of the student. Does he or she feel comfortable with this facility? The teacher can also try both conditions, with support and without support, sometime before the examination and establish what is best in terms of results.

● *Will a child who is diagnosed with dyslexia grow out of it?*

The simple answer to this question is 'No'. Children, however, are continually developing and areas that are problematic when they are 7 may not be a problem at 17. That is not to say that the young person has 'grown out' of the problem, but he or she may have compensated for the difficulty by utilising personal strategies.

● *How can you tell the difference between a poor speller and a dyslexic child?*

Firstly, not all children with dyslexia are poor spellers and, of course, there are many people who are poor spellers who are not dyslexic. It is important to recognise that there are a number of characteristics of dyslexia, and poor spelling may be only one of these. There are, however, some fairly classic dyslexic-type spelling errors, some of which are shown in Figure 7.1. But I would emphasise that other factors associated with dyslexia would also be noted. Having said that, it is possible for young people with dyslexia to compensate and develop skills that can deal with their dyslexic difficulties but may still have an obvious difficulty in spelling. It can be difficult for children to unlearn established patterns of spelling. That is why they can habitually make the same mistakes time and time again.

● *If my child is diagnosed with dyslexia, should I give up on him or her entering tertiary education?*

Absolutely not: there is no reason why children and young people cannot fulfil their potential. Tertiary education needs to ensure that they have the accommodations in place to cater for the needs of students with dyslexia. It is best for the student to make contact with the college well before the course starting date. This will help the college to plan for the accommodations that are necessary. Additionally, it is also important that the student discloses his or her dyslexia on the application form. It

- 'y' endings, such as in 'deny' and 'reply', may be spelled as 'denie' and 'replie'.
- Double consonants, such as 'suggestion' and 'beginning', are often spelled as 'sugestion' and 'begining'.
- Vowal digraphs, such as 'ie', as in 'review', are often spelled 'reveiw' or 'reveu'.
- Word endings, such as 'tion' as in 'fraction', can be spelled as 'fracsion'.
- 'ent' or 'ant' endings can be mixed; for example, 'different' and 'constant' can be spelled 'differant' and 'constent'.
- Silent 'e' words, such as 'whistle' and 'save', may have the 'e' omitted.
- Beginning sounds, such as 'wh' as in 'which' and 'whistle', can be spelled as 'wich' and 'wistle'.
- Phonetic spellings may be used for irregular words, so 'whistle' may be spelled 'wistel' or 'whistel'.
- The use of the letters 's' and 'c' can be confused: 'absence' can be spelled as 'abcense'.
- Plurals can be difficult: 'buses' and 'cups' can be spelt as 'busses' and 'cupes'.
- Words that sound the same can be misspelled, as in 'weak' and 'week', 'knight' and 'night' and 'their' and 'there'.
- Other examples can include: 'weeck' for 'week', 'lick' for 'like', 'gim' for 'gym', 'reding' for 'reading', 'langwig' for 'language', 'wey' for 'way', 'scoll' for 'school', 'breyke' for 'break', 'frends' for 'friends', etc.

Figure 7.1   Some characteristic spelling errors

is also important that this period should be as stress free as possible and good communication between the student and the university (usually the disability department) is essential.

- *If my child requires a scribe and reader for examinations, how will the child cope with a job when he or she leaves education?*

This is a good question. Similar supports should be available in tertiary education but ideally the student should be encouraged to minimise the support used. That is to say that readers, in particular, should only be used if absolutely necessary.

In the workplace the employer has to make accommodations for individuals with dyslexia. This may mean that materials can be provided in taped rather than printed form. But in terms of self-esteem and the individual's own morale, it is always best to try to become as independent as possible and to develop strategies to deal with difficult situations. But it is also important to remember that support is there and it is the right of people with dyslexia to ask for and access that support.

Parent responses: parents can be dyslexic

One of the many parents from New Zealand who responded to the questionnaire suggested that, as dyslexia usually runs in families, it is very likely that one of the parents will have the same processing style as their dyslexic son or daughter. In some situations this can present a difficulty. But, as this parent pointed out, it need not. The parent commented on how the family can have fun with the dyslexic thinking style and in fact treat it as the 'norm' – this would make such a style an asset and not a deficit.

A parent from Queensland, Australia, said that she needed to start up her own dyslexia support group because there was no information or knowledge of dyslexia in the small town where she lived. She found assistance, however, from a lady within the District Education Office who had a child who is dyslexic and provided a great deal of support and advice, particularly on how to deal with the school. It is not too unusual now for teachers or education officials to either know someone with a dyslexic child, or in fact to have a dyslexic child themselves. This can be very helpful to parents and particularly if they can successfully engage these people and persuade them to join support groups. This parent in Queensland, like so many other parents, found out a great deal about education and about dyslexia – this, she suggests, has helped her to deal with schools more effectively and has provided information on how best to help her son. One of the pitfalls highlighted by this particular parent is that of the dyslexic child becoming too dependent on the parent. When this view was expressed by the teacher to this parent, the parent replied: 'Yes, he does rely on me because I am the only one who really understands how he struggles. He said, "Mum, you are the only one who can explain my dyslexia to me so that I can understand it."' The important point is to strike a balance. As this parent suggested: 'Yes, he will rely on me to a certain extent, but he will also be embarrassed to have his mum at school helping him, so I will help him by showing him how to look at things in different ways until he can work it out himself.' What seemed to come across in the response from this parent was the energy expended into ensuring that her dyslexic child was adequately assessed and that the classroom intervention was appropriate. In situations like this it is often a parent who informs the school, and the parent is usually the best source of information on dyslexia for the school. If this is the case, schools need to accept this and harness the parent's energy and knowledge in a positive and constructive manner. Such parents can be excellent contributors to school boards or become very effective teacher aides.

Summary of parents' responses

Q1 *What are the factors that made it difficult for you as a parent of a child with dyslexia?*
- concern over the demanding school environment
- remembering poems/stories and parts for plays
- reading
- frustration with educational services and understanding the school system
- failure of education services to pay for private assessment
- lack of clarity on methods and approaches in dealing with dyslexia
- always have to take the initiative and inform schools of new developments in dyslexia
- getting your child past the 'I'm dumb' label that such children tend to give themselves
- obtaining an assessment in the first instance
- having to explain to every secondary school teacher about your child's dyslexia.

Q2 *From whom did you get your support?*
- relying on friends and family
- internet
- other parents
- the school.

Q3 *What strategies did you, as a parent, use to help to support your son or daughter with dyslexia ?*
- private tuition

- using games at home as a learning tool
- infinite patience
- sense of humour
- empathy
- taking things at their pace not mine
- loads of positive feedback
- breaking down tasks into the smallest component parts.

Summary

This chapter has outlined some of the concerns and anxieties of parents directly from parents themselves. One of the striking points is that parents often have to take the initiative and many have done this very successfully. It is also apparent that some parents have benefited from good communication with the school and dialogue with teachers who are knowledgeable on dyslexia. Nevertheless, parents can have a number of anxieties relating to the extent to which their child can reach his or her potential. Modern society places many demands on parents, and parents of children with dyslexia can have demanding life situations that can be very stressful (Lednicka, 2004). Lednicka found this to be the case in her research study that involved interviewing sixty-two families in the Czech Republic. While this is understandable, she also acknowledged that there is scope for some optimism as it is now well known that there is a positive side to dyslexia and it is important that this is recognised and harnessed.

Many of the points in this chapter, although emanating from parents who responded to a questionnaire, are applicable to all parents and can also be generalised to parents in different countries. The message is the same for all: be positive and optimistic.

Chapter 8

Alternative approaches

One factor that seems to characterise the field of dyslexia, and, indeed, other specific learning difficulties, is the incessant flow of innovative treatments that claim to promise a cure. These so-called 'cures' can be misleading. At the same time, however, they should not be discounted and need to be examined seriously. One of the other characteristics about these innovations or cures is that they usually cost money and the target market is normally parents. Schools are unlikely to adopt a new approach if it has not been tried and tested.

This is therefore a very important chapter for parents as they will often be at the vulnerable end of the vigorous marketing of a new product or treatment. It is important that parents are aware of these new products and treatments, are able to judge their value and can weigh the potential benefits against the costs.

The most frequently asked questions at parent meetings usually relate to new treatments. This was mentioned in the previous chapter. Larry Silver made an interesting general comment on such innovations in an article, 'Controversial therapies', in the International Dyslexia Association periodical *Perspectives* (Summer 2001). Silver suggested that, understandably, parents of children with learning disabilities are susceptible to anyone offering a treatment approach that will 'cure' or 'correct' the problems, often in a brief period of time. The interesting point is that although these treatments are seen by professionals as controversial, the people offering these treatments are usually very busy with many clients. This indicates that parents will pay money if they think a treatment can offer them, and their child, something that the school cannot provide, and promise an end to the difficulties associated with dyslexia.

Why controversial?

These 'treatments' are controversial because usually any new approach goes through a process of implementation, evaluation, revision and re-evaluation and the results of these developments are usually written up in respectable, academic, peer-reviewed journals. This means that when a research exercise on a new approach is concluded, the researchers send a report in the form of an academic article to a journal for publication. The journal editors then send it to several other academics working in the same field for comment. The journal editors are seeking advice on whether the submission reaches the academic standards of the journal and, particularly, if the research has been soundly and rigorously carried out. This peer review is standard practice and many of the innovations and cures around today have not been peer reviewed in this way. Usually the practice of accepting a new idea is slow and can take many years as it has to go through this rigorous research and peer-review process.

Some of the new cures are based, initially at least, on an individual's 'hunch' and these may be reported in newspapers capturing usually sensational headlines and a large potential audience. When this happens parents often want more information on these cures. They would normally seek information from the source of the innovation because the school will seldom have knowledge of these 'cures'. Education authorities tend to use only those methods that have been tried and tested. Naturally these sources are not independent and would normally quote research conducted by its own staff or clients.

Silver suggests that an approach is considered controversial if it is proposed to the public before any research is available, and if the proposed approach goes beyond what the research data supports. This highlights the fact that parents need to obtain as much information as possible about a new approach before they spend money on such remedies.

The rest of this chapter will provide a summary of some of these alternative treatments as well as some principles that parents need to consider before buying into them.

Visual approaches

There are a number of different visual treatments that have been specifically marketed for treating dyslexia. Most are commercially operated and run by private companies, although some have close links with universities and other research establishments.

Scotopic sensitivity

This term was first used in 1983 when Helen Irlen presented a paper on Scotopic Sensitivity Syndrome at the annual meeting of the American Psychological Association. She proposed that tinted glasses would improve the reading ability of dyslexic children and, following that paper, the treatment became popularised and sensationalised before there was time for sufficient control studies to be carried out to verify the claims (Silver, 2001). Scotopic sensitivity, which is now more commonly referred to as Meares–Irlen Syndrome, refers to the presence of a visual defect that can be related to difficulties with light source, glare, wavelength and black and white contrast. Irlen, in fact, reported on a number of areas of difficulty, such as:

- Eye strain
- Poor visual resolution
- Reduced span of focus
- Impaired depth perception
- Poor sustained focus.

The assessment procedures for the above are usually carried out though a screening process by people who have undergone courses to become screeners. Some optometrists also carry out such screening. During the screening the individual is asked a series of questions after being shown pages containing different patterns, musical notes, geometric figures and words. Observations are then made on the individual's responses. For example, observations will be made on the length of concentration span, whether the figures jump, run off the page, merge and if vision is blurred when concentrating on complex visual images. The colour of any lenses that are prescribed are usually determined by the responses to these factors as well as some additional and more sophisticated laboratory procedures.

Helveston (2001) suggests that much of the supporting evidence for the success of visual treatments is anecdotal. At the same time the treatment has been very popular and many recipients have claimed that the treatment has been successful. Arnold Wilkins, a scientist with the Medical Research Council (Wilkins, 2003), clearly supports the notion of visual stress and produced a sophisticated screening device which he called the Intuitive Colorimeter – an instrument that measures the degree of therapeutic tint. Wilkins has performed a number of controlled scientific studies to examine the effectiveness of the use of tinted glasses following assessment using the Intuitive Colorimeter (Wilkins et al., 1996; Scott et al., 2002). Wilkins also demonstrates the benefits of coloured lenses in individuals with migraine headaches (Wilkins et al., 2002).

Different systems: consensus or confusion

There are a number of systems in use to diagnose visual stress and/or prescribe coloured glasses. These include the Irlen system, the Intuitive Colorimeter system (Wilkins), the ChromaGen™ system, TintaVision© and Optim-Eyes™.

According to Wilkins (2003), no technical data on the precision of the tints using the Irlen or the ChromaGen™ systems are available. The ChromaGen™ system comprises special filters designed for the management of visual dyslexia. ChromaGen™, however, has produced a series of extensive and very promising in-house studies using a larger number of clients. One of these studies refers to the results of the application of the ChromaGen Haploscopic filters to 434 dyslexic individuals. The author claims that there was a 91% success rate based on comparisons of both reading and writing skills from before the lenses and three months after continuous wear of the ChromaGen™ lenses. Similarly, Harris and MacRow-Hill (1998) reported gains in colour vision and in rate of reading using ChromaGen™ contact lenses with young people with dyslexia.

It is difficult and confusing for parents to decide, firstly, whether the expense of embarking on a visually based treatment for dyslexia is valid, and, secondly, if they do wish to embark on that kind of treatment, which practice offers the best hope and has the most supportive evidence of success.

Although they operate on similar principles, there are differences in how each of the systems has developed. Each system will provide glowing and accurate case studies highlighting the success of the intervention. For example, Wilkins (2003, p. 129) provides a number of supportive comments from users such as

> my youngest son John is now 12. He recently came home from school quite upset as he had forgotten to take his lenses into an exam and unfortunately had found difficulty in reading the questions. ... Later in class he reread the questions with his lenses and realised just what a difference they did make to him. (Parent)

Similarly, ChromaGen™ report (CSD 234, Issue 1, March 2003) on an account of a drama student who was having severe difficulties in reading and learning scripts and was also unable to coordinate her actions on stage because of resulting stage fright. After using ChromaGen™ lenses in both eyes her rate of reading increased and her word retention improved dramatically. She said: 'Overall I am more confident and able to project myself with text reading' (p. 3). The *Yorkshire Evening Post* in the UK carried a story (22.10.03) showing how an 11-year-old boy had amazed family and teachers 'with a stunning turnaround in his academic perfomance' after wearing ChromaGen™ glasses for six months.

Coloured overlays

Some children may benefit from the use of coloured overlays. These are less expensive than tinted glasses and can be changed more readily. Usually it is best if the child has a complete set of overlays as the most effective colour can change according to the lighting conditions. The colour used at home can be different from that used in school. Arnold Wilkins (2003) explains that the colour selected by the child for an overlay may be different from that used in glasses. This is because of the light process – the light has to pass through the overlay once to reach the paper and again after reflection from the paper. Wilkins suggests that this increases the saturation of the colour. Additionally, the state of adaptation of the eyes differs for overlays and lenses. Overlays provide a surface colour and are viewed through white light, while lenses have a similar effect to coloured light, everything in the visual field is coloured. Wilkins suggests that around 1 in 5 of all children in mainstream school will benefit from coloured overlays, and that 1 in 20 will derive considerable benefit by reading more than 25% faster with overlays. Certainly, overlays can be an accessible way for the child to use colour to help with reading. They can be relatively cheap and easy to carry around.

Visual dyslexia

There is a great deal of research now to support the notion of visual dyslexia. There is research looking at the role of the Magnocellular visual system (Stein, 2004), which is a peripheral visual system and is particularly sensitive to light flicker and high contrast. This can result in words becoming blurred when reading and using eye-tracking motion. Ian Jordan, an optician with a special interest in visual dyslexia, suggests that treatments should aim to reduce, or modify, the visual stimulus and this can be done by improving the lighting, taking care with the layout of text and through the use of colour to reduce contrast and pattern glare (Jordan, 2002).

Another type of visual difficulty that children may display is that of convergence. This occurs when both eyes cannot meet at a point close enough to read accurately, which means that the child will have difficulty in fixation and may get double vision. Jordan suggests that the treatment for this type of difficulty can be achieved through masking one eye, visual exercises, use of colour and prescription glasses.

Optim-Eyes™

Jordan suggests that the best way of achieving the most comfortable colour is through the use of the Optim-Eyes™ task light. This is a practical lamp that can be used for reading and writing, and has flexible positioning. The light is designed to switch on and off individual colour receptors in the retina, as this allows for the best balance between colours. Jordan does maintain, however, that a significant level of expertise is required from the person assessing the problem and applying the treatment. He advocates that for best results it should be used in conjunction with the Jordan Reversal and Inversion Test and the Jordan Pattern Glare Screening Test in order to set the optimum colour balance for each individual's needs.

Asfedic Tuning

A company called TintaVision has developed a sophisticated form of Asfedic Tuning. Asfedia is a condition of the visual system where the cells in the retina are not properly in tune, and according to Irons (2004) this can result in a range of slight to severe difficulties in reading normal black on white text backgrounds. TintaVision has tested over 4,000 individuals in this way, and Irons, the research director of the company, suggests that the expected outcome is an improvement in reading speed and reading accuracy. In the UK, Asfedic Tuning is approved for use by the Students Support Division in Higher Education although it has not yet been extensively used in mainstream education. TintaVision suggests that the use of Asfedic Filters and the colour coordinates for a few weeks produces a physical change in the eye, and this change improves reading ability. It also means that the exact colour required for further improvement also changes and subsequent tuning sessions should be seen as a 'top up'. The company suggests that, in general, people need around three tunings.[1]

Comment

There is now much more evidence to support the view that dyslexia can have a visual basis. This has led to a number of developments and innovations in relation to colour, eye movement and visual acuity in general. These innovations need to be taken seriously although the research basis is, to some extent, anecdotal. Nevertheless, many users of the various colour systems claim significant improvements through

[1] www.tintavision.com

its use, and this cannot be ignored. Additionally, some of the treatments are not too expensive – coloured overlays being the least expensive and readily obtained.

If parents feel that their child has some visual disturbance that is affecting his or her reading, then the first port of call should be the local optician. The optician may not be fully aware of the systems discussed above – although some opticians are offering such services – but can certainly provide expert advice on the state of your child's vision. Opticians can easily identify more common factors such as convergence, erratic eye movement and tracking difficulties as well as provide a full health check on the eyes. The systems mentioned above, however, need to be carefully considered as users claim significant success and such accolades should not be too readily dismissed. Additionally, all those involved in the systems discussed above are making great efforts to develop their mechanisms scientifically and are endeavouring to support these developments with controlled research studies. Further studies can pave the way for these innovations to become more widely used and more widely appreciated.

Fatty acids and supplements

There is a very strong view – much of it arising from the research conducted by Richardson (2001) and others – that certain fatty acids play an important role in the development of the eye and brain coordination in learning ability, concentration and memory. They suggest that there is now growing evidence on the important role of Highly Unsaturated Fatty Acids (HUFA) of the omega-3 and omega-6 families. They report that about 30% of the dry weights of the eye and brain are made up of these vital nutrients. Furthermore, they can only be obtained through dietary sources. They also suggest that the industrialisation of the food chain – with an extension to the shelf life of most foods – has resulted in the dietary removal of these nutrients. Some green leaf vegetables, as well as nuts and seeds, can provide the parent LNA omega-3 fatty acid which then has to be metabolised before it can be utilised by the body. The researchers suggest that fish oil supplements or oily fish and seafood can give a more direct input of these nutrients.

The latest research indicates that omega-3 is very important and trials in schools in Durham in the north of England[2] show that the use of Hi-EPA supplementation can improve the learning abilities of children with dyslexia, dyspraxia and ADHD. Dr Madeleine Portwood, lead author of the trial, stated that

> for some children on the trial we saw dramatic improvements in reading ability; as much as four or five years in some cases . . . in terms of handwriting we also saw marked differences. Their confidence and self-esteem also improved . . . and many of the children who were previously excitable and hyperactive found themselves able to concentrate.
>
> (Equazen Nutraceuticals, 2004, p. 6)

The research also indicates that fatty acids delivered in their most natural bio-available form have greater efficacy than the processed or synthetic form. Further, the research also indicates that the right blend of omega-3 and omega-6 fatty acids has a positive effect on brain-cell signalling.

Comment

There is little doubt that healthy bodies and healthy minds are important for learning. Healthy children will be more alert and more able to concentrate and attend for longer periods. There is also little doubt that food additives and the processes involved in the food chain today can be detrimental to the intake of vitamins and other natural sources from food. Additionally, many fast foods that are consumed by children may be deprived of the supplements discussed in the fatty acid research debate. All the pointers seem to indicate that nutrition is vital for learning and that children with some form of learning difficulty can be most at risk. It makes sense, therefore, to take this seriously. It is also encouraging that the manufacturers and the researchers involved in fatty acid supplements have commissioned a number of controlled studies and have developed their products continuously over the years in the light of this and other scientific research.

[2] www.durhamtrial.org

Other dietary treatments

There are a number of other dietary and ingestive treatments that claim to have some success with people with learning difficulties. These can include megavitamins and trace minerals, glyconutritional supplement and herbal remedies. There may well be some validity in these claims but if parents are considering using these with their children they should, according to Arnold (2001), refer to the following factors:

- Is there research data comparing the treatment to a control condition?
- What is the age and diagnosis of the children who have responded to the treatment?
- What are the risks and expenses involved?

Additionally, Arnold suggests that parents should try to log the results by rating the child's performances before and after the treatment in as objective a way as possible. He suggests that if results are not obvious after a reasonable period of time, it may be wise to move on to another treatment.

It is also important to acknowledge that some treatments, such as herbal remedies, should be tried only under supervision, or at least with your medical practitioner's knowledge, especially if other drugs are being taken at the same time.

The Davis Dyslexia Correction Method®

This method is an example of an approach that has been subjected to both heavy criticism and great acclaim at the same time. The approach is described in full in the book *The Gift of Dyslexia* by Ronald D. Davis and Eldon M. Braun which was first published in 1994 and revised in 1997. The two key aspects of this programme are symbol mastery and orientation/disorientation. Davis suggests that people with dyslexia experience disorientation from an early age and this disorientation in the brain affects the ability to read print. The other factor in the Davis method relates to symbol mastery – that is, what the symbol looks like and what the symbol means. The difficulty, according to Davis, is that people with dyslexia think in pictures and symbol mastery infers verbal conceptualisation, which implies the need to think with the sounds of language. He suggests in his book that we need to 'keep in mind that dyslexics have little or no internal monologue, so they do not hear what they are reading unless they are reading aloud' (Davis & Braun, 1994, rev. 1997, p. 12). It appears that the contrast between verbal and non-verbal conceptualisation that the dyslexic person experiences when reading can cause confusion and, according to Davis, this results in disorientation. This 'means that the perception of the symbols gets altered and becomes distorted so that reading and writing is difficult or impossible' (p. 14).

The intervention consists of an intensive programme carried out by individuals specifically trained in this method. The programme includes symbol mastery sessions, orientation counselling and spell–reading exercises. The programme also includes fine-tuning exercises to help the individual find his or her optimum orientation point and coordination therapy. The book also contains a number of key words that can trigger disorientation.

In his book, Davis defines dyslexia as

> a type of disorientation caused by a natural cognitive ability which can replace normal sensory perceptions with conceptualisations; reading, writing, speaking or directional difficulties which can stem from disorientations triggered by confusions regarding symbols. Dyslexia stems from a perceptual talent.
>
> (Davis & Braun, 1994, rev. 1997, p. 244)

It must be stated that this is a controversial definition of dyslexia – it may not be totally inaccurate because dyslexic individuals may have a visual perceptual talent, though not always, but they will usually experience confusions with reading symbols. Most of the research body on dyslexia views dyslexia as a phonological and/or visual difficulty – which are the core difficulties, and the principal interventions need to focus on these areas. Additionally, children and adults with dyslexia may differ in how they are affected by dyslexia, so it makes sense to view each individually. Different interventions may be needed for different types of dyslexic difficulties. Cicci (2001) believes that there is little research literature to support the orientation and disorientation theories and that the actual teaching to read or teaching to learn are absent from the Davis methods. At the same time, Marshall (2003) suggests that studies show that conventional methods of teaching reading may be sufficient for the majority of children but can be counterproductive when used with dyslexic children. She suggests that the Davis Dyslexia Correction Method®, with an emphasis on modelling words on clay, can help to build the mental pathways that brain-scan evidence shows to be crucial for reading development among dyslexic students.

Exercise and movement

There has been a long-standing interest in exercise and therapies based on movement for children with dyslexia and other specific learning difficulties. Doman and Delacato (Tannock, 1976) developed a series of exercises related to motor development and this has been developed considerably by Blythe (1992), Blythe and Goddard (2000), Goddard-Blythe and Hyland (1998), Dobie (1996) and McPhillips et al. (2000). Some of these are discussed below.

The inhibition of primitive reflexes

Blythe (1992) found that 85% of those children who have specific learning difficulties that do not respond to various classroom intervention strategies have a cluster of aberrant reflexes. He argues that as long as these reflexes remain undetected and uncorrected, the educational problems will persist.

These reflexes should only be present in the very young baby and would become redundant after about six months of life. But Blythe suggests that if these reflexes continued to be present after that time, the development of the mature postural reflexes will be restricted and this will adversely affect writing, reading, spelling, copying, maths, attention and concentration.

Blythe (1992) and Goddard-Blythe (1996) have developed the Developmental Exercise Programme – an assessment and intervention programme for assessing the presence of these reflexes – and a series of exercises designed to control the primitive reflexes and release the postural reflexes. This view, regarding the affect of uninhibited primitive reflexes on learning, has been supported by other studies.

Details of this programme can be obtained from the Institute for Neuro-Physiological Psychology (INPP).[3]

The INPP have been responsible for pioneering research into NeuroDevelopmental Delay (NDD) and its impact on specific learning difficulties, including dyslexia, dyspraxia, ADD, ADHD and DAMP (Dysfunction of Attention, Motor, Perception). They have centres in many countries including Scotland, Ireland, the Netherlands, Sweden, Germany, Finland and Italy.

McPhillips et al. (2000) suggested that foetal movements which form the basis of the INPP reflex inhibition programme (Blythe, 1992; Goddard-Blythe, 1996) may play a critical role in the maturational processes of the development of the infant's brain and this can have implications for cognitive development and subsequent skills involved in, for example, the reading process. In fact, Goddard-Blythe and Hyland (1998) found birth complications as the single most significant factor in children who later went on to develop specific learning difficulties. In a study in Western Australia, Taylor (2002), in view of the work of Blythe and Goddard-Blythe referred to above, examined the effects of retention of primitive reflexes in children diagnosed as ADHD. Her results supported the evidence of the importance of this area for cognitive development and learning.

Educational kinesiology

Educational kinesiology is a combination of applied kinesiology and traditional learning theory, although some aspects of yoga and acupressure are also evident in the recommended programme.

Kinesiology is the study of muscles and their functions, and particular attention is paid to the patterns of reflex activity that link effective integration between sensory and motor responses. It has been argued (Mathews, 1993) that children often develop inappropriate patterns of responses to particular situations and that these can lock the child into inappropriate habits.

[3] www.inpp.org.uk

Dennison and Hargrove (1986) have produced a series of exercises (Brain Gym®) from which an individual programme can be devised for the child relating to the assessment. Many of these exercises include activities that involve crossing the mid-line, such as writing a figure eight in the air or cross-crawling and skip-a-cross, in which hands and legs sway from side to side. The aim is to achieve some form of body balance so that information can flow freely and be processed readily. This programme, known as Brain Gym®, has been widely and successfully implemented in the school setting (Fox, 1999; Longdon & Longdon, 2001, 2004; Taylor, 1998). Dennison and Dennison (1989, 2000) developed a system called Brain Organisation Profile (BOP) to visually represent their theory. Taylor (2002) examined the basis and application of this profile with children with ADHD. She was able to develop a useful brain organisation profile for each child in the research sample and found that children with ADHD did show more evidence of mixed laterality processing than the control group.

Dyslexia, Dsypraxia and Attention Treatment

DDAT is the name given to the exercise-based treatment (Dore & Rutherford, 2001) based on the cerebellar deficit (Fawcett & Nicolson, 2004; Nicolson et al., 2001). This theory implies that the cerebellum has an important function in relation to dyslexia and other learning difficulties. The treatment programme also implicates other aspects of neurological/biological development, such as the functioning of the magnocellular system, the inhibition of primitive reflexes and fatty acid deficiencies. Dore and Rutherford suggest that the cerebellum maintains its plasticity throughout childhood and therefore it is theoretically possible to retrain the cerebellum to function more efficiently. The resultant Balance Remediation Exercise Training Programme assesses the vestibular and cerebellar functioning and implements a series of exercises directly related to the individual profile of each child following a series of sophisticated tests using an electronystagmography system for assessing eye movement and a posturography balance system. Controlled studies that have sought to provide clinical evaluation of the

DDAT have been implemented and reported (Reynolds et al., 2003). These results were encouraging, and indicated that after six months' treatment the clients showed physiological changes with substantial improvement in vestibular function, visual tracking and fundamental cognitive skills.

In a commentary to this report in *Dyslexia* (May 2003), however, Snowling and Hulme outlined what they considered to be numerous methodological and statistical problems with the study and concluded that it 'provides no evidence that DDAT is an effective form of treatment for children with reading difficulties' (Snowling & Hulme, 2003, p. 127). Stein, in the same edition of the journal, suggested that he believed that

> there is evidence to support the hypothesis that the development of the cerebellum is mildly impaired in dyslexics; hence their postural control, balance and eye control may be compromised and therefore treatment designed to improve these might help dyslexics.
>
> (Stein, 2003, pp. 124–125)

Stein goes on to say, however, that this study did not meet the gold standard set for scientific studies. This means that studies should be double blind and randomised with control groups. Despite this, and other critical comments made on the research paper (Singleton, 2003), Nicolson and Reynolds (2003, p. 174) suggest that their results are sound and indicate that 'they have undertaken all the further tests suggested by commentators and these have served merely to confirm the original pattern of results'.

There is no easy solution to the dilemmas faced by parents who have the means, and wish to do their best for their child. Certainly DDAT will work for some children but for others it may not – which is the risk attached to any intervention, particularly new ones. The wisdom of Tim Miles, a highly regarded and long-standing figure in the dyslexia field, is worth acknowledging when he says

> when I used to talk to worried parents, some of whom were willing to spend their last penny to help their dyslexic child and they enquired about a form of treatment which I believed to be controversial or dubious, I

did not actively discourage them, but I urged them and the child to be aware of possible disappointments if the treatment did not work.

(Miles, 2003, p. 122)

The Mozart Effect

There has been a great recent interest in the role of music in learning. This has been referred to as the Mozart Effect (Anderson et al., 1999). They suggest in their book, *Learn with the Classics: Using Music to Study Smart at any Age*, that Mozart music with its rhythms, melodies, harmonies and high frequencies primes the brain to perform more effective brain activity. This can be beneficial for most types of learning, including mathematical thinking. The authors suggest that Mozart music shares the same brain patterns as some types of complex brain activities and that Mozart music actually exercises the brain and causes new brain connections to be made and new pathways to be formed.

This is an interesting view and one that has been adopted in a number of schools, such as the Red Rose School, for Dyslexic Children in St Anne's on Sea in Lancashire, England. Additionally, it is relatively inexpensive and can give pleasure to others in the family.

Other accelerated learning techniques

There is a considerable range of books and approaches based on the premise of accelerated learning. These maintain that this approach can help children with dyslexia. Some of these, such as Mind Mapping®, are well established and are very much seen now as mainstream and a very acceptable and successful strategy.

Some others, however, can be gimmicky and promise great gains in a short period of time. There are some points that parents may wish to consider in relation to these, such as appreciating that the strategy must be suited to the learner and whether the method will be helpful for the subjects the learner is studying. If you come across a study skills strategy that you think may be helpful, you should discuss this with the school first, or try it out yourself. One of the important considerations is the child's actual learning style. This was discussed in Chapter 3 and can influence the success or otherwise of a strategy.

Learning styles and alternative interventions

As was indicated in Chapter 3, there are a number of different ways of learning. Each person has to a certain extent a unique way of absorbing, understanding and remembering information. Similarly, there are a number of different types of learning styles, and these can be divided into cognitive and environmental.

'Cognitive' means how information is processed, which can be done

- visually
- auditorily
- kinaesthetically
- in a tactile (touch) manner.

Learners may use a combination of these, but often have a preference, and parents will easily recognise the style that best suits their child. Some children, of course, can accommodate very well to different learning situations and may have several preferences.

Factors within the 'environment' can influence the effectiveness and the efficiency with which we learn. Environmental factors discussed in Chapter 3 include aspects such as

- sound – music and other background sounds can affect learning
- lighting – some children prefer to work in bright lights while others prefer a dim light such as a small table
- furniture and design – which refers to the preference some children have for informal seating and seating arrangements such as working on a sofa rather than using a desk and chair.

Although it is acknowledged that they can have differences, children with dyslexia do tend to be global, visual and kinaesthetic. This means that they will learn best when information is presented visually and need to have the 'whole picture' available and explained to them when learning. They will also normally learn best through the experience of learning.

The child's learning style, therefore, may have an impact on the success or otherwise of an intervention or therapy. Irrespective of the intervention or therapy used, it is beneficial to consider the child's learning style and learning preferences before selecting a method.

Comment on alternative treatments

There are many views on the validity of alternative programmes of treatment. These programmes are usually not harmful, and, indeed, those reported here may hold much promise. Many of these may appear different but actually may arise from similar casual concerns relating to the neurological/biological developmental processes and, indeed, may be complementary to each other. It is important, however, that the enthusiasm over any particular treatment or intervention does not minimise the effect of good classroom teaching. There is an abundance of well-researched teaching and learning programmes and strategies used in schools that have been developed following years of practice and research. Parents need, initially at least, to put their trust in the school. If they wish to pursue any alternative programme, this can also be discussed with the school as the chances of success will be greater if the parents and school are working in partnership – even in relation to an alternative and controversial intervention.

Certainly the theoretical justifications of various approaches are important, as are treatments supporting the foundations of learning, such as those reported here, but it is also important to strive for a comprehensive view and multidisciplinary approach to supporting children and adults with dyslexia and other learning difficulties. Without collaboration and cooperation between all the professionals involved in seeking to help people with learning difficulties and differences, confusion, concern and anxiety will arise and can reach exaggerated proportions. Interestingly, in 2002 the organisation Dyslexia in Scotland found it necessary to send to all its members a special fact sheet on an alternative approach because of the questions raised by parents. This informative fact sheet did much to present the facts, which clearly was what the members wished. An interesting and reflective comment, however, was made by the authors in the conclusion to the fact sheet:

> Dyslexic adults we have spoken to don't want a cure they simply want an improvement in their literacy skills and their organisational skills. They do not want to lose their special gifts.
>
> (Dyslexia in Scotland, 2002, p. 4)

There are many other alternative treatments that have not been discussed in this book. Some of these are popular with parents, such as Sound Therapy (Johanson, 1997), which is based on frequency-specific left-hemisphere auditory stimulation with music and sounds (Auditory Discrimination Training) and many others – often too many for the parent or teacher to handle or understand. This further underlines the need for collaboration between parents and professionals – perhaps the approach that always works is called 'effective communication'.

Summary

This chapter does not necessarily advocate that parents should seek out and buy into any of the alternative approaches mentioned here. Ideally, the school should have the resources and the expertise to meet the needs of your child. Realistically, however, there will be variations between counties throughout the country, with some schools and authorities being highly geared up to deal with dyslexia and others not. Nevertheless, parents must always see the school as the best hope of helping their child to achieve success. If the parents feel that the school is not adequately equipped, then they should discuss this with the school head teacher. If parents do wish to access any of the therapies mentioned in this chapter, they should see them as supplementary rather than as a substitute for the intervention that takes place in school.

Chapter 9

Information: a personal need – a global concern

Each child with dyslexia is unique. This means that the needs, requirements and supports for parents may differ. It is for this reason that local contacts can be extremely valuable. These include local support groups and parent associations as well as the local school. The importance of the local school has been indicated many times throughout this book and the school should be the first line of information. It is very possible, however, that the school may not have the source of information and support that is required by parents. In fact, many parents I have spoken to while undertaking research for this book indicated that the opposite may be the case. The school may find out about recent developments in dyslexia from the parents. That, of course, varies; but the power and influence of parents as sources of information on dyslexia for the school, and for other parents, should not be underestimated. The fact that a number of teachers are also parents of children with dyslexia is also helpful and in such cases the school can often be more informed than one would expect on dyslexia. Teacher aides and teaching assistants can also be very well informed about dyslexia and some may also be parents of a dyslexic child.

Parent associations have a key role to play in pooling resources and disseminating information on dyslexia through open evenings, websites, leaflets and conferences. In fact, in some instances parent groups have undertaken work that should be carried out in school. For example, in New Zealand, SPELD offers an educational service to parents in both assessing and tutoring children with dyslexia. In Hungary, the organisation Startdyslexia undertakes assessments, teaching and preparation of materials for children with dyslexia, including pre-school children. There is evidence that if the service is not available, parents will take the initiative and provide it themselves. A number of successful schools have been set up by parents and by members of the community to help to meet the specific needs of children with specific difficulties. One such school is the highly successful Discovery School in Christchurch, New Zealand.

Because dyslexia is a continuum and can overlap with other conditions, parents and parent support groups can link constructively with other related organisations, some of which are listed below. The list is by no means exhaustive – the world wide web provides a ready source of information on dyslexia for parents. If anything, there is so much confusing and conflicting information around that parents have to be selective in what they access and should always consult others before embarking on a programme, especially a costly one, for their child. Again, the school could and should be a source of advice. It is understood that this is not always the case; however, dyslexia associations are widespread and accessible.

Parents are also keen to complement the work of the school by pursuing a literacy programme at home. This can sometimes be successful but it is always best to receive some guidance from the school. A selection of resources that may be useful for parents is shown below.

There are also examples of contacts that can be useful for parents but it should be emphasised that these are only a sample and parents should access websites and materials that relate to their own geographical area and school system.

Books

Ann Arbor Publications

www.annarbor.co.uk

This company produces a number of resources, most of which focus directly on literacy skills. In relation to written expression the resource

'Teaching Written Expression' may be useful. This programme offers a theoretical framework and a practical step-by-step guide to developing sentences, constructing paragraphs, editing and developing a 'sense of audience'.

Before Alpha: Learning Games for the Under Fives

B. Hornsby (1996)
Souvenir Press, London

This book contains a number of learning games that can be used with children under five. These games are in a series of structured stages, are multi-sensory and aim to foster language development and other pre-reading skills such as visual and auditory perception and discrimination, fine motor control, spatial relationships, knowledge of colour, number and directions.

Developmental Dyspraxia: A Practical Manual for Parents and Professionals

Madeleine Portwood (1996)
Durham County Council, Educational Psychology Service, County Hall, Durham

This manual is illustrated and appropriate for both parents and teachers. The first two chapters provide a neurological oriented background but without the learning terminology that usually accompanies such explanations. These chapters are followed by a chapter entitled 'What is dyspraxia?' This provides a summary from 6–12 months to 7 years describing some observable behaviours found in dyspraxic children. The definition that the author uses to describe dyspraxia is located in this chapter: 'motor difficulties caused by perceptual problems, especially visual-motor and kinaesthetic motor difficulties' (p. 15).

The following chapters look at assessment of the junior age child, attainment tests, cognitive assessment and screening. The rest of the manual focuses on remediation programmes for different age groups. The book concludes with addresses and contacts for parents and teachers.

Dyslexia: Parents in Need

Pat Heaton (1996)
Whurr, London

This book describes some of the responses from parents in answer to research questions affecting parents of dyslexic children. It deals with aspects such as early signs, language difficulties, parents' feelings and perceptions, practical aspects and factors influencing effective liaison with the school.

Section two of the book contains over 20 pages of word searches and other game-type activities for identifying vowels and consonants.

Dyslexia in Practice: A Guide for Teachers

Janet Townend and Martin Turner (Eds) (1999)
Kluwer Academic Publishers, Kingston upon Thames

This book has been produced with contributions from experienced practitioners from the Dyslexia Institute. There are chapters on phonological awareness, spoken language, the bilingual dyslexic child, linking assessment with a teaching programme, the teaching of basic reading and spelling, developing writing skills, learning skills, mathematics, the use of ICT (information and communication technologies), the challenges facing dyslexic adults and linking home and school.

Dyslexia: A Practitioner's Handbook (3rd edition)

Gavin Reid (2003)
John Wiley & Sons Ltd, Chichester

This book provides a comprehensive view of dyslexia. It has chapters on identification, assessment, teaching and learning. There is also information for parents and chapters on bilingualism, adult dyslexia and inclusion.

Dyslexia: Successful Inclusion in the Secondary School

Lindsay Peer and Gavin Reid (Eds) (2001)
David Fulton Publishers, London

Although this book is aimed at teachers, it can be of interest to parents and there is a chapter, written by Angela Fawcett, outlining her experiences as a parent. This book provides an overview of the potential impact of dyslexia in the secondary school and shows how subject teachers can deal with this in different subject areas. There are chapters on modern foreign languages, English, history, geography, physics, biology, general science, mathematics, art, drama and music.

Failure to Connect: How Computers Affect our Children's Minds – For Better or Worse

Jane Healy (1998)
Simon & Schuster, New York

This is a fascinating book that unravels the 'glitz and novelty' of computer technology and the impact it has on learning and on children's health. This is a constructive book that can help children to use technology effectively and provides sound advice to parents in particular. Jane Healy explains the difficulties and dangers faced by parents and suggests that 'in the case of the child under seven there are few things that can be done better on a computer and many that fail miserably by comparison' (p. 218). In this book Dr Healy investigates the effects of computer technology on all possible areas affecting the child – social, cognitive, emotional and personal. Jane Healy is also the author of the popular *Your Child's Growing Mind* (1994), Bantam Doubleday, New York.

Get Ahead: Mind Map$^©$ your Way to Success

Vanda North with Tony Buzan (2001)
Buzan Centres, England

This book presents a colourful introduction to the use of mind maps and highlights the use of colours in learning and suggestions on how to use mind maps for activities such as note-taking, learning symbols, planning and speaking to groups. This is very suitable for all students but particularly those with a dyslexic processing style who may find it very useful for preparation for examinations.

Get Better Grades

Maggie Agnew, Steve Barlow, Lee Pascal and Steve Skidmore (1995)
Piccadilly Press, London

This short text on study skills looks at attitude, organisation, listening and note-taking, reading and writing skills and revision for exams. The information is presented in an eye-catching manner and contains study strategies more suitable for older children and even some adults.

Helping Children with Reading and Spelling: A Special Needs Manual

R. Reason and R. Boote (1994)
Routledge, London

This manual consists of teaching plans incorporating a range of strategies intended for use with children who have difficulty learning to read, write and spell. It contains a considerable number of strategies and some of these can be carried out at home.

How to Teach your Dyslexic Child to Read: A Proven Method for Parents and Teachers

Bernice A. Baumer (1996)
Birch Lane Press, Carol Publishing Group, New Jersey

This book describes an intensive one-to-one teaching programme that includes charts, graphs and lesson plans. The programme is aimed for the child from kindergarten through to third grade in a step-by-step procedure. It provides detailed instructions on teaching phonics, spelling and syllables. There are also examples of word lists and other exercises focusing on initial consonants, vowels, blends and diphthongs.

Language Shock: Dyslexia across Cultures

A Multimedia Training Pack for learners, parents and teachers
European Children in Crisis (ECIC)
Dyslexia International – Tools and Technologies (DITT)
Rue Defacqz 1, B–1000, Brussels, Belgium

This package was created to provide a European-wide perspective of dyslexia and particularly the needs of staff in European multicultural, multilingual schools. The package contains a detailed guide, a video and a website. The package was developed by European Children in Crisis, which is a non-profit, non-governmental organisation to help to promote the interests of children with learning difficulties.

The guide is very informative and is divided into three sections. The first section, on understanding dyslexia, includes chapters on dealing with dyslexia and bilingualism and dyslexia. The other two sections are on 'dealing with dyslexia', which contain chapters on assessment and chapters specially written for teachers and for parents. The guide also provides details relating to further information that may be useful for parents and teachers. There is a chapter on children's rights and resources and contacts. This contains details of European-wide organisations and a summary of the education system and educational initiatives in 17 member states.

Laughing Allegra

Anne Ford with John-Richard Thompson (2004)
Newmarket Press, New York
www.newmarketpress.com

This is the story of a mother's challenges for her daughter, Allegra, confronted by severe learning disabilities. Informative and compelling, it tells how the mother, Anne Ford, desperate for answers, sought out countless schools, doctors and tutors for help. Anne tells of how she faced rejection, intolerance and puzzlement from many professionals and friends. The book also includes sections on commonly asked questions, a resource guide and the challenges facing mothers in this situation.

This story is from the heart and the reader is soon caught up in the plights and the successes shared by Allegra and her mother. The realism of sharing your life with a person with LD is encapsulated in the author's comment: 'What I did not realise was that learning disabilities are not confined to the classroom and that the problems of the spring would follow us deep into the summer. Learning disabilities do not take vacations' (p. 46). This is a book about how learning disabilities can be dealt with in learning, leisure, family and education.

Learning Styles: A Guide for Teachers and Parents

Barbara Given and Gavin Reid (1999)
Red Rose Publications, St Anne's on Sea, Lancashire
www.dyslexiacentre.com

This book provides a critical analysis of learning styles and insights into the five learning systems: emotional, social, cognitive, physical and reflective. It also offers practical applications of an interactive observational checklist for identification of preliminary individual learning styles.

Living with Dyslexia

Barbara Riddock (1996)
Routledge, London

This book provides an overview of dyslexia from a range of perspectives, including educational, emotional, social, parent, teacher and children. There is a chapter dedicated to case studies. The book is essentially the product of a research project conducted by the author and one of the aims of the book is to examine how information on living with dyslexia can be collected in a systematic manner, and integrated with other forms of research to increase one's understanding of dyslexia.

Another aim of the book is to raise constructive debate on the advantages and disadvantages of using the label 'dyslexia'. Essentially, the author provides a broader perspective of dyslexia, indicating that it is more than just a reading disability.

Lost for Words: Dyslexia at Second Level and Beyond
A Practical Guide for Parents and Teachers

Wyn McCormack (1998)
Tower Press, Dublin

This book focuses on the Republic of Ireland education system. It is written from a parent–teacher perspective, and provides a descriptive account of how dyslexic children may progress through the system. It particularly relates to how parents can help their child at second level and beyond, and gives advice on how to cope with administration, career choice and accessing support services. Contextualised within the Irish Republic, it describes services offered by specific colleges and details aspects of school policy. There are also sections on strategies for presenting and coping with different subject areas.

Praxis Makes Perfect

Dyspraxia Trust, PO Box 30, Hitchin, Herts SG5 1UU

This publication contains nine chapters, all on areas concerning dyspraxia. Dyspraxia is defined as an 'impairment or immaturity in the organisation of movement which leads to associated problems with language, perception and thought'. There are, therefore, chapters on understanding dyspraxia and views from teachers, psychotherapists and occupational therapists. The book contains guidance on dealing with handwriting problems, advice on activities for dyspraxic children and general considerations at school, including social integration in the classroom.

Spelling and Spelling Resources

Pete Smith, Mike Hinson and Dave Smith (1998)
NASEN Publications, Tamworth

This book is divided into two areas: one on the teaching of spelling, assessment, approaches and policy and the other on resources that can be used for spelling, including an index of spelling resources as well as examples of software programs and useful websites. There is also an annotated list of materials on spelling with an indication of the suitability level.

Stride Ahead: An Aid to Comprehension

Keda Cowling (2001)

This book can be a useful follow up to *Toe by Toe*. Essentially, *Stride Ahead* has been written for children who can read but may have difficulty in understanding what they are reading. *Stride Ahead* is available from Keda Publications, 17 Heatherside, Baildon, West Yorkshire BD17 5LG. Tel./fax: 01274 588278.

Teaching Reading and Spelling to Dyslexic Children

Margaret Walton (1998)
David Fulton Publishers, London

This practical A4-size book begins with a description of different reading approaches and strategies that can be used for dyslexic children. The remainder of the book focuses on a teaching programme beginning with the alphabet, then sounds and blends. There are also activities on punctuation, spelling and finding suitable books as well as photo-copiable resources in the appendix.

The Dyslexia Handbook

BDA, 98 London Road, Reading RG1 5AU

This very informative handbook is published annually and always contains practical strategies and advice on dyslexia and other associated difficulties, such as dyspraxia and attention difficulties.

It contains sections on general information about dyslexia, including definitions, adult dyslexia, identifying dyslexia, articles for parents and a directory of addresses of relevant local and national dyslexia associations. Usually there are sections on legislation and computers.

The Gift of Dyslexia. Why Some of the Smartest People Can't Read and How They Can Learn

Ronald D. Davis with Eldon M. Braun (1994)
Ability Workshop Press, Burlingame, CA

This book describes a specific approach on tackling dyslexia, devised and indeed experienced by the author. The author describes dyslexia as a type of disorientation, similar to the type of disorientation one experiences sitting in a motionless car, when a car moves alongside. The author therefore sees dyslexia from a perceptual perspective and the programme described in the book emphasises the role of perception. The exercises, which are part of the programme 'Davis Orientation Mastery', describe perceptual ability assessment, basic symbol mastery and symbol mastery for words.

The International Book of Dyslexia: A Guide to Practice and Resources

Ian Smythe, John Everatt and Robin Salter (2003)
John Wiley & Sons, Ltd, Chichester

This book provides information on research, policy and practice on dyslexia from around the world together with details of dyslexia associations and resources. Over 50 countries are included in this extensive book, which also has an electronic supplement.

Together for Reading

Dorothy Smith, John Shirley and John Visser (1996)
NASEN Publications, Tamworth

The theme of this book is teachers and parents and the authors' views are expressed throughout indicating that parents have an important role in helping their child to develop reading skills. This short book (48 pages) contains suggestions on the importance of parental involvement, home–school communication, organising a partnership scheme, sections on staff development and examples of workshops that could be used to assist the teacher–parent partnership. There is an appendix that contains checklists for involving parents in reading, a summary of legislation and some suggested strategies for decoding unknown words.

What To Do When You Can't Learn The Times Tables

Steve Chinn (1996)
Marko Publishing

This is a practical book aimed at providing strategies to help dyslexic students to learn tables. It is not intended to be a quick-fix book and each of the methods suggested requires practice and perseverance. It suggests that the use of a table square is a more efficient method than learning the tables through a linear collection of facts. The book contains ideas to minimise the memory load on the dyslexic student and to provide strategies which with practice can help the dyslexic student to become a more efficient and successful learner in mathematics.

Adult books

Dyslexia in Adults: Education and Employment

Gavin Reid and Jane Kirk (2001)
John Wiley & Sons, Ltd, Chichester

This book gives some insights into the issues relating to dyslexia in adults in study and in the workplace. It begins by discussing some of the issues that have relevance to this group, such as the use and misuse of labels, support in the workplace, assessment availability, the use of the term 'disability', the screening process, the use of technology accessing resources and learning style. There are also chapters on screening, assessment and support, training, dyslexia in the workplace, learning strategies and chapters focusing on both the negative and positive consequences of the dyslexia experiences. This is echoed in a chapter that allows dyslexic adults to recount their own experiences. There is a final chapter on sources of support and resources.

Dyslexia: Students in Need

Pat Heaton and Gina Mitchell (2001)
Whurr, London

This book offers some practical advice on study skills and examinations. The book contains a number of detailed and practical appendices. There are also chapters on study skills, survival techniques and resources and assessment.

The Adult Dyslexic: Interventions and Outcomes

David McLoughlin, Carol Leather and Patricia Stringer (2002)
Whurr, London

This comprehensive book provides a wealth of information on dyslexia in the adult years. There are excellent chapters on interventions, identification, counselling, personal development, literacy for life, academic and professional skills, careers, the workplace and advocacy. These chapters discuss in detail all the demands that can be placed on adults with dyslexia and how such demands can be dealt with. The book contains a wealth of practical advice.

The Dyslexic Adult in a Non-Dyslexic World

Ellen Morgan and Cynthia Klein (2000)
Whurr, London

This book looks at the world of dyslexic adults based on their own personal perspectives and experiences. The book also examines cognitive styles and diagnosis as well as support issues, family and work and career aspects.

Programmes

Phonological Awareness Training: A New Approach to Phonics

Jo Wilson (1993)
Educational Psychology Publishing, University College, London

This is a specific programme on a particular aspect of literacy development–phonological awareness. The programme complements other types of activities such as stories, poems and rhymes which are beneficial to the development of phonological awareness. The essential component of PAT is the use of analogies to help children to read and spell.

The programme consists of 25 worksheets, reading lists, dictation sheets and 'rime' display sheets. The programme can be used with an individual child or with a group and is suitable for children of 7 years and upwards.

Spelling World

Amanda Gray (1994)
Nash Pollock Publishing, Oxford

A photo-copiable spelling programme that contains a series of 4 books at different levels based on the look, cover, write, check principle. Covers

500 of the most commonly used words and contains a range of activities to help with spelling and integrated handwriting activities.

Step into Phonics: A Structured Guide for Sequential Phonics

Lois Lindsay and Corey Zylstra (2001)
Learning Takes Two, 5888 Olympic Street, Vancouver, BC, Canada V6N 126
www.stepintophonics.com

This excellent resource contains 120 easy to follow lessons with appendices on short vowel words list for the beginning reader; a copy of the Dolch basic vocabulary with 220 phonetic and non-phonetic words; sight word vocabulary lists and word exceptions to rules. There are also complementary materials available such as working sheets, phonogram ideas, short vowel cards and finger puppets.

THRASS®

www.thrass.com

The Teaching of Handwriting, Reading and Spelling Skills, known as THRASS®, can be useful and has many different aspects that can be accessed by children and parents. Details of these can be found in the comprehensive THRASS® webpage.

Toe by Toe: Multisensory Manual for Teachers and Parents

Keda and Harry Cowling (1999)
Available from Toe by Toe, 8 Green Road, Baildon, West Yorkshire BD17 5HL
Tel. 01274 598807

'Toe by Toe' is a multi-sensory teaching method highly recommended for teachers and parents. The programme has a multi-sensory element, a phonic element, some focus on the student's memory through the planning and the timing of each of the lessons in the book. It can be readily used by parents and the instructions are very clear.

Interactive literacy games

Crossbow Education

41 Sawpit Lane, Brocton, Stafford ST17 0TE
www.crossboweducation.com

Crossbow Education specialises in games for children with dyslexia and produces activities on literacy, numeracy and study skills. These include 'Spingoes', an onset and rime spinner bingo which comprises a total of 120 games using onset and rime, and 'Funics', a practical handbook of activities to help children to recognise and use rhyming words, blend and segment syllables, identify initial phonemes and link sounds to symbols. 'Funics' is produced by Maggie Ford and Anne Tottman and is available from Crossbow Education. Crossbow also produces literacy games including Alphabet Lotto, which focuses on early phonics, 'Bing-Bang-Bong' and 'CVC Spring', which help to develop competence in short vowel sounds and 'Deebees', which is a stick and circle board game to deal with b/d confusion.

They also have board games called 'Magic E Spin-it' and 'Hot-words' – both five-board sets, the first for teaching use of 'e' spellings and the second for teaching and reinforcing 'h' sounds such as 'wh', 'sh', 'ch', 'th', 'ph', 'gh' and silent 'h'. 'Oh No' is a times table photo-copiable game book, and 'Tens 'n' Units' consists of spinning board games that help children of all ages to practise the basics of place value in addition and subtraction. Many of these activities are simple and fun to use and can be easily accessed by parents for home use.

Games and practical activities are also available from:

Multi-Sensory Learning

www.msl-online.net

This company provides a range of games and activities for reading, spelling and numeracy. It also has software and a number of kits and games called memory boosters. The memory boosters include a pock-etbook of reading and spelling reminders, signs and symbols, Lotto, line tracker, high-frequency and key words, happy families for great spelling and word search activities. These are all highly motivating and colourful and have a high interest level. It also produces a structured reading and spelling programme.

Smart Kids (UK) Ltd

5 Station Road, Hungerford, Berkshire RG17 0 DY
Fax: 01488 644 645; tel.: 01488 644 644

This company produces the eye-catching and highly colourful smart phonics series of activities. These include games and activities on developing consonants, vowels and digraph beginnings for kindergarten, followed by a sequence of packs for different levels focusing on blend beginnings and endings, magic 'e' vowel digraphs and changeable vowel sounds. The activities have supplementary materials using poetry cards, magnetic whiteboards and whiteboard markers, foam magnetic letters in seven colour groupings, picture sound magnets and spelling and sound cards. The company also has a branch in Auckland, New Zealand.

Phonic resources

Many of the teaching programmes for children with dyslexia are based on phonics. Some other phonic resources that may be of interest to parents include:

- *Active Phonics Workbooks* (Ginn & Company)
- *Finger Phonics* (Jolly Learning Ltd)
- *Phonic and Phonic Resources* (NASEN)
- *Phonic Links* (Collins)
- *Rhyme and Analogy* (Oxford University Press)
- *Sounds Easy* (Egon Publishers)
- *Sounds Patterns and Words* (Collins)
- *Step into Phonics* (Learning Takes Two)
- *Stile Early Phonics* (LDA)
- *The Big Book of Early Phonics* (Prim-ed Publishing)
- *The First Phonic Blending Book* (Kickstart Publications)
- *The Phonics Bank* (Ginn & Company)
- *The Phonics Handbook* (Jolly Learning Ltd).

Computer programs

TextHelp©

The program known as TextHelp© is particularly useful for assisting with essay-writing. TextHelp© has a read-back facility and a spell-checker that includes a dyslexic spell-check option that searches for common dyslexic errors. Additionally, TextHelp© has a word prediction feature that can predict a word from the context of the sentence, giving up to ten options from a drop-down menu. Often dyslexic students have a word-finding difficulty and this feature can therefore be very useful. This software also has a 'word wizard' that provides the user with a definition of any word; options regarding homophones; an outline of a phonic map; and a talking help file.

Inspiration

'Inspiration' is a software program that can help to develop ideas and to organise thinking. Through the use of diagrams it helps the student to comprehend concepts and information. Essentially the use of diagrams can help to make creating and modifying concept maps and ideas easier. The user can also prioritise and rearrange ideas, helping with essay-writing. 'Inspiration' can therefore be used for brainstorming, organising, pre-writing, concept mapping, planning and outlining. There are 35 in-built templates and these can be used for a range of subjects including English, history and science. Dyslexic people often think in pictures rather than words. This technique can be used for note-taking, for remembering information and organising ideas for written work. The Inspiration program converts this image into a linear outline.

www.r-e-m.co.uk

This company provides a comprehensive catalogue of software for use with children with dyslexia. Programs include: Starspell, Wordshark 3, Clicker 4 (this enables students to write with whole words and pictures), TextHelp© read and write, Penfriend (able to predict words before they are typed), Wordswork (uses a learning styles approach), Inspiration (for creative planning and brainstorming), Numbershark, Times Tables and Parenting Snakes and Ladders.

IANSYST Ltd

This company provides computers and technology for helping dyslexic people of all ages at college, school, work or home. It also provides products such as TextHelp©, Dragon Naturally Speaking, Inspiration and software on learning skills such as reading, spelling, grammar, comprehension and memory. Websites: www.iansyst.co.uk and www.dyslexic.com.

Crick Software

www.cricksoft.com

This popular clicker program can be used for sentence building, word banks, writing frames and multimedia. Lively presentations, e.g. the series 'Find out and write about' includes programs on explorers, castles and animals. It also provides Clicker books and Clicker animations.

Don Johnston Special Needs

www.donjohnston.co.uk

This provides a host of early literacy interventions and multimedia books to reinforce early literacy learning. This company provides the popular Start-to-Finish books – a high interest, controlled vocabulary series that are particularly suitable for reluctant readers. It also provides talking word processor programs such as Write : Outloud and Co : Writer 4000.

Organisations and sources of information

- **Adult Dyslexia Organisation (ADO)**
  336 Brixton Road, London SW9 7AA
  Helpline: 0171 924 9559

- **Arts Dyslexia Trust**
  www.sniffout.net/home/adt
- **British Dyslexia Association**
  98 London Road, Reading RG1 5AU
  Helpline: 0118 966 8217; admin: 0118 966 2677; fax: 0118 935 1927
  helpline@bda-dyslexia.demon.co.uk   or
  admin@bda-dyslexia.demon.co.uk
  www.bda-dyslexia.org.uk
- **Canada Dyslexia Association**
  www.dyslexiaassociation.ca

This association has produced an extremely interesting article titled 'Voices of Dyslexia: Tragedies and Triumphs,' which is available on their website. It provides illuminating accounts of the obstacles that some individuals have had to overcome. For example, one of the accounts from a computer expert, aged 50, who is a senior civil servant, reveals how he was told he could not learn when he took a second language course. He was tested for dyslexia only two years ago and has had to overcome many hurdles in life without realising why he was experiencing difficulties. He said, 'The more you know yourself, the better you become at something, and that is the one thing that should be the centrepiece of your life's work.' There is also an account by a senior official of the Canadian government, aged 54, who hid her disability until three years ago when she told staff and actually received a lot of respect from colleagues and employees.

The article also contains advice for parents, encouraging parents to accept dyslexia and suggesting that the problem is 50% solved with your recognition and acceptance. There are also tips for employers of people with dyslexia.

- **Council for the Registration of Schools Teaching Dyslexic Pupils (CReSTeD)**
  Greygarth, Littleworth, Winchcombe, Cheltenham GL54 5BT
- **Department for Education and Employment (DfEE)**
  Sanctuary Buildings, Great Smith Street, Westminster, London SW1P 3BT
  Tel.: 0171 925 5000; fax: 0171 925 6000
  www.dfee.gov.uk

- **Dr Gavin Reid's website**
  www.gavinreid.co.uk
- **Dyscovery Centre**
  Multi-disciplinary assessment centre for dyslexia, dyspraxia, attention deficit disorders and autistic spectrum disorders
  www.dyscovery.co.uk
- **Dyslexia Association of Ireland**
  Suffolk Chambers, 1 Suffolk Street, Dublin 2
  info@dyslexia.ie
- **Dyslexia Institute**
  www.dyslexia-inst.org.uk
- **Dyslexia Research Trust**
  www.dyslexic.org.uk
- **Dyslexia Scotland**
  Unit 3, Stirling Business Centre, Wellgreen Place, Stirling, Scotland
  FK8 2DZ
  Tel.: 01786 446 650; fax: 01786 471 235
  www.dyslexiascotland.com
  Also Dyslexia Ayrshire: www.dyslexiayrshire.org.uk
- **Helen Arkell Dyslexia Centre**
  Frensham, Farnham, Surrey, UK
  www.arkellcentre.org.uk
- **Hornsby International Centre**
  Wye Street, London
  www.hornsby.co.uk
- **International Dyslexia Association**
  8600 LaSalle Road, Chester Building, Suite 382, Baltimore, MD
  21286-2044, USA
  Tel.: (410) 296 0232; fax: (410) 321 5069
  info@interdys.org; www.interdys.org IDA
- **National Association of Special Educational Needs (NASEN)**
  www.nasen.org.uk
- **Northern Ireland Dyslexia Association**
  7 Mount Pleasant, Stranmilis Road, Belfast BT9 5DS
  www.nida.org.uk
- **Red Rose School**
  28–30 North Promenade, St Anne's on Sea, Lancashire, England, UK
  www.dyslexiacentre.com

- **www.dyslexia.uk.com**
  For more information about your child's dyslexia.
- **www.dyslexia-teacher.com**
  Provides a wealth of information for teachers and parents world wide, on materials, books and courses. Runs course on training for teachers and parents in the teaching of children with dyslexia. The course has students from 48 countries and is very practical based.
- **www.dyslexics.org.uk**
  Suggestions for parents, things that can be carried out at home.

Publishers/Products/Services

- **Ann Arbor**
  Fax: 01668 214484
  www.annarbor.co.uk
- **Better Books**
  3 Paganel Drive, Dudley DY1 4AZ
  Tel.: 01384 253276; fax: 01384 253285
  www.betterbooks.com
- **Canada Dyslexia Association**
  290 Picton Avenue, Ottawa, Ontario
  cda@ottawa.com; www.dyslexiaassociation.ca
- **Creative Learning Company, New Zealand**
  www.creativelearningcentre.com
- **Crossbow Education**
  41 Sawpit Lane, Brocton, Stafford ST17 0TE
  www.crossboweducation.com
- **Dyslexia Parents Resource**
  www.dyslexia-parent.com
- **Family Onwards**
  www.familyonwards.com
- **Fun Track Learning Centre**
  Perth Western Australia (Mandy Appleyard, Educational Consultant)
  Offers full assessment and tutoring services for children ages 5–16 and consultancy to parents and schools
  mappleyard@funtrack.com.au   www.funtrack.com.au

- **IANSYST Ltd**
  The White House, 72 Fen Road, Cambridge CB4 1UN
  www.iansyst.co.uk   and   www.dyslexic.com
- **John Wiley & Sons Ltd**
  Tel.: 0800 243407 (UK) and + 44 1243 843294 (overseas); fax: +44 (0) 1243 843 296
  www.wileyeurope.com
- **LDA: Literacy Resources for Special Needs**
  Fax: 0800 783 8648
  www.LDAlearning.com
- **Learn with the classics** and other books on the use of learning with music
  www.lind-institute.com
- **Learning Works International Ltd**
  9 Barrow Close, Marlborough, Wiltshire SN8 2BD, UK
  Provides a range of materials for children to enhance learning. Some excellent materials and activities on memory work. Also publishes excellent book on Dyscalculia by Anne Henderson, Fil Came and Mel Brough.
  www.learning-works.org.uk
- **Lucid Research Ltd**
  3 Spencer Street, Beverley, East Yorkshire HU17 9EL, UK
  Provides memory booster software, a stimulating and fun way to improve children's memory skills.
  www.lucid-research.com
- **Mind Genius Ygnius; Gael Ltd**
  SE Technology Park, East Kilbride, Scotland G75 QOR
  Helps to write mind maps and convert to different forms of text.
  Tel.: 01355 247766
  www.mindgenius.com
- **Multi-Sensory Learning (MSL)**
  www.msl-online.net
- **Paired Reading**
  www.dundee.ac.uk/psychology/TRW
- **Phonic and Phonic Resources**
  Mike Hinson and Pete Smith (1997) NASEN (available directly from NASEN House)

- **REACH**
  Orton–Gillingham Learning Center, 121A–123 East 15th Street, North Vancouver, BC, Canada V7M 1R7
  www.reachlearningcenter.com
- **SEN Marketing Dyslexia and Special Needs Bookshop**
  618 Leeds Road, Outfield, Wakefield WF1 2LT
  Tel./fax: 01924 871697
  info@sen.uk.com; www.sen.uk.com
- **Special Needs Assessment Profile (SNAP)**
  C. Weedon and G. Reid (2003) Hodder & Stoughton
  www.snapassessment.com – section for parents on website
- **TextHelp$^{©}$ New Zealand**
  www.heurisko.co.nz/texthelp
- **Texthelp Systems Ltd**
  Enkalon Business Centre, 25 Randalstown Road, Antrim BT41 4LJ, Northern Ireland
  Tel.: + 44 1849 428 105; fax: +44 1849 428 574
  info@texthelp.com; www.texthelp.com
- **The Mystery of the Lost Letters**
  A tri-lingual, self-help tool for dyslexic learners and their mentors.
  www.ditt-online.org
- **The School Daily**
  5 Durham Street, Box 8577, Christchurch, New Zealand
  Provides a wealth of useful and update information on education and dyslexia.
  Fax: +64 3 366 5488
  www.The SchoolDaily.com
- **Western Australia – Dyslexia Educational and Psychological Services**
  Wells House, Suite 2, 35 Hay Street, Subiaco, WA 6008
  Provides assessment and support for people with learning problems, run by Shelley Farrow, Registered Psychologist, member of the APS.
  Tel./fax: (08) 9387 4054
  www.s.farrow@bigpond.net.au
- **Whurr Publishers Ltd**
  19b Compton Terrace, London N1 2UN
  Tel.: 0171 359 5979; fax: 0171 226 5290

- **Xavier Educational Software Ltd**
  www.xavier.bangor.ac.uk

Other specific learning difficulties

Attention deficit disorders

- ADHD books: www.adders.org and www.addwarehouse.com
- ADHD behaviour management: www.StressFreeADHD.com
- ADHD diet: www.feingold.org
- Attention Deficit Disorder Association: www.chadd.org   and
  www.add.org
- Dyscovery Centre (Multi-disciplinary assessment centre for dyslexia, dyspraxia, attention deficit disorders and autistic spectrum disorders): www.dyscovery.co.uk
- The National Attention Deficit Disorder Information Service:
  www.addiss.co.uk

Developmental coordination disorders/dyspraxia

- Dyspraxia Foundation: www.dyspraxiafoundation.org.uk
- Dyspraxia Connexion (website offers support, information and practical help: www.dysf.fsnet.co.uk
- Mindroom: charity aimed at helping children and adults with learning difficulties: www.mindroom.org
- QuEST therapies: www.questtherapies.com
- www.dyspraxia.org.nz
- www.hiddenhandicap.co.uk

Autistic spectrum disorders. Asperger's syndrome

- National Autistic Society: www.nas.org.uk
- www.futurehorizons-autism.com

Speech and language difficulties

- Afasic: www.afasic.org.uk
- I CAN: www.ican.org.uk
- www.childspeech.net
- www.talkingpoint.org.uk

Summary

This chapter relates to the local needs of parents by providing them with advice on the type of books that are available and websites where information can be accessed. There is a considerable range of resources available and this chapter has only highlighted a small section of these. Irrespective of the country, there are, therefore, resources available, or certainly resources that can be ordered through the internet. The local needs of parents have the potential to be satisfied. Local support groups can also help with this, but what is very concerning is the wide disparity in provision for, and indeed acceptance of the needs of, children with dyslexia. This is a global concern. In time, most countries will eventually provide in some way for dyslexia. It can be dangerous, costly and wasteful of the countries' potential to ignore it.

Concluding comments

Choices and decisions

Support

The information in Chapter 9 can certainly help parents to make informed decisions and access as much support as is necessary. Yet one of the features that emerged from the research conducted for this book was that many parents still feel alone and unsupported. Perhaps the most valuable source of support for any parents is the school, and if, for some reason, the school is not supportive, then they may well feel alone, even if other areas of support are available.

It is reassuring that teacher education programmes on dyslexia have gained momentum in recent years. There are many excellent examples from the UK (Reid, 2001) of education programmes in dyslexia, and an increasing number of courses are being accredited by the British Dyslexia Association. In the USA, there is a similar increase in teacher awareness and the International Dyslexia Association at its annual conference always has speakers on teacher training on the programme. Support, therefore, should eventually come from the school but parents have a choice if it is not.

Schools

Increasingly, parents have a choice over schools. This choice applies to both the state sector as well as the private independent sector. Parent power has increased considerably and, in a democracy, schools are ultimately accountable to the government elected by the people. Parents should not be unwilling to seek advice from their elected representative and, in my experience, this avenue often does bring about change and results. Having said that, I realise this is not always the case. I received a response from a parent in New Zealand who said 'we received no government support for our child and schools are not designed for dyslexic children'. The writer of this response may well have a point, but having engaged with government officials in many countries I know that there is a willingness to listen and to make change that will benefit all. It is important that parents are involved directly and indirectly in such change.

Nevertheless, parents may well decide to opt out of the state system and enrol their dyslexic child in a private school. Again, they have choices to make as there is a wide range of facilities among the private sector and some schools accommodate to dyslexia more than others. There are some schools that are only for children with dyslexia and for some children this may be the short-term (or even long-term) answer. Most of these schools are residential, but some do have a local catchment area and are day schools. One such provision for children with dyslexia in the UK (Red Rose School, www.dyslexiacentre.com), which was discussed in an earlier chapter, has opted for a day school model while many others in the UK and the USA offer residential accommodation. (A full list of residential schools for children with dyslexia can be found in *The BDA Handbook*, published annually.)

What should parents look for in a school?

It is important that the child feels comfortable in the school, so naturally the child should accompany the parents on school visits. Some of the questions parents should ask include:

- How easy will it be to communicate with the school? What system does the school have in place for communication with parents? This should be made clear at the outset.
- What type of training have the staff had on dyslexia? Has the training involved only a few teachers or has there been whole staff awareness training?
- Is there any special provision for children with dyslexia in the school?
- If there is, what programmes and strategies does the school use? Can parents link with these programmes at home?
- Will my child have full access to the curriculum? What are the compulsory subjects?
- What is the school's homework policy?
- Are classes streamed?
- How many children with dyslexia does the school teach? If the answer is 'very few', then it may be that the school does not recognise or identify dyslexia – but usually most teachers will have had some experience of children with dyslexia.
- What is the school policy on dyslexia? How are the teachers informed of that policy?

Careers/subject choice

This essential issue was discussed in Chapter 6. It is important to re-iterate that no career should be out of the question and it is crucial that the young person realises this at an early age. It is also important that, together with the school and your child, you can identify his or her strengths as these can help to identify the type of courses that would be most suitable in further and higher education. Most courses now require a degree of reading and writing, but some have less than others. At the same time, however, it is important that the young person chooses the course that he or she wants to do. For example, it is not uncommon for students with dyslexia to select English Literature as their main subject at university even though they may have more reading to do.

One of the key points about subject course and career choice is to seek advice and to obtain it well ahead of time. Many careers advisers now have more awareness of dyslexia, but if they do not, you can provide them with information.

Final comments

Parenting is not an easy task. Parenting a child who has additional needs, whatever these may be, can be doubly difficult. It is often the case, however, that with dyslexia the parents at least understand the difficulty. Because it runs in families, parents may have dyslexia or it may have afflicted one of their relatives. This can help with an understanding of the difficulty and can help parents to appreciate exactly what it is like to experience dyslexia. The challenge facing parents is to ensure that children and young people with dyslexia can become resilient so that when they are faced with difficult situations, they can believe in themselves and in their abilities. They need to become aware of their own potential and strengths and have the confidence and motivation to tackle new learning in new situations. Education, after all, should be a training for life, not for reading. Certainly reading is important, but there are ways and methods of overcoming the barriers that people with dyslexia can experience with print. Teachers, schools and education systems need to incorporate dyslexia fully into their training of teachers and consider the needs of students with dyslexia in curriculum planning and in target setting. Already in many, but not all, countries much has been done to help students with dyslexia in examinations. This needs to be carried through to all areas of learning so that dyslexia is considered and catered for in all schools in every country. Only then will parents be able to feel confident about the prospects of their dyslexic child.

We are fortunate that within the field of dyslexia there are some well-established and successful parent organisations that have been instrumental in bringing about change. There are also some very sympathetic governments and education departments who recognise the needs of children with dyslexia. There are many committed teachers who have sought out information and training in dyslexia so they are equipped to understand and support the children with dyslexia in their classrooms. There are many prominent researchers seeking answers to the questions on the causes and characteristics of dyslexia that can help to inform understanding and practice. There are also many parents and parent groups who have campaigned vigorously and passed on their experience to other parents. The situation is promising, yet for some, perhaps many, the situation is bleak. They feel unsupported, alone, confused and desperate. What is needed is for the good practice to become the norm, good intentions to become reality, dissemination to be widespread and a system that is sympathetic. Above all, parents need understanding – they more than anyone know their child, and need to be listened to.

In writing this book and in recording some of the significant successes that parents and parent organisations have made, I am reminded of the fact that parents are parents, not campaigners, or pioneers. Parents' priorities lie in the home with the family and the family network. Both the child and the family have to live with the reality of dyslexia every day. Bad experiences can be enduring and have a significant effect on family life. The emotional side of dyslexia needs to be appreciated by all.

This book has tried to portray most of the key actors that parents will encounter and tried to guide parents through the dilemmas they may face and decisions they may have to make. But we should not lose sight of the fact that although the book is about dyslexia, we are, in effect discussing children and individuals – children with everyday needs and everyday hopes. It is our responsibility as parents, as educators, as employers or as citizens of the community to ensure that these needs are met and that these hopes are kept alive.

References

Anderson, O., Marsh, M. & Harvey, A. (1999) *Learn with the Classics. Using Music to Study Smart at Any Age*. San Francisco, CA: LIND Institute.

Arnold, L.E. (2001) Ingestive treatments for learning disorders. *Perspectives*, **2** (3), 18–20.

BDA (annually) *The Dyslexia Handbook*. Reading: British Dyslexia Association.

Blythe, P. (1992) *A Physical Approach to Resolving Specific Learning Difficulties*. Chester: Institute for Neuro-Physiological Psychology.

Blythe, P. & Goddard, S. (2000) *Neuro-physiological Assessment Test Battery*. Chester: INNP, 4 Stanley Place.

Buzan, T. (1993) *The Mind Map Book – Radiant Thinking*. London: BBC Books.

Castles, A., Datta, H., Gayan, J. & Olson, R.K. (1999) Varieties of developmental reading disorder: Genetic and environmental influences. *Journal of Experimental Child Psychology*, **72**, 73.

Cicci, R. (2001) *The Gift of Dyslexia* by Ronald D. Davis: A critique. *Perspectives*, **27** (3), 10–11.

Clark, K. (Ed.) (2004) *Count Me In. Responding to Dyslexia*. Scotland: University of Strathclyde.

Crombie, M. & Schneider, E. (2003) *Dyslexia and Modern Languages*. London: David Fulton Publications.

Crombie, M., Knight, D. & Reid, G. (2004) Dyslexia: Early identification and early intervention. In G. Reid & A. Fawcett (Eds) *Dyslexia in Context: Research, Policy and Practice*. London: Whurr.

CSD 234 (2003) *ChromaGen*™ *Report*, Issue 1 (March). Cantor & Nissel Ltd. www.cantor-nissel.co.uk

Dargie, R. (2001) Dyslexia and history. In L. Peer & G. Reid (Eds) *Dyslexia: Successful Inclusion in the Secondary School*. London: David Fulton Publications.

Davis, R.D. & Braun, E.M. (1994, revised 1997) *The Gift of Dyslexia. Why Some of the Smartest People Can't Read and How They Can Learn*. London: Souvenir Press.

Dennison, G.E. & Dennison, P.E. (1989) *Educational Kinesiology: Brain Organisation Profiles*. California: Edu-Kinesthetics Inc.

Dennison, G.E. & Dennison, P.E. (2000) *Educational Kinesiology: Brain Organisation Profiles. Teachers' Training Manual* (3rd edn). California: Edu-Kinesthetics Inc.

Dennison, P.E. & Hargrove, G. (1986) *Personalized Whole Brain Integration*. California: Edu-Kinesthetics Inc.

Department for Education (1944) Education Act (1944). HMSO.

DfES (1994, revised 2001) *Special Education Needs Code of Practice*. London: Department for Education and Skills.

Dobie, S. (1996) Perceptual motor and neurodevelopmental dimensions in identifying and remediating developmental delay in children with specific learning difficulties. In G. Reid (Ed.) *Dimensions of Dyslexia*. Edinburgh: Moray House Publications.

Dore, W. & Rutherford, R. (2001) *Closing the gap*. Paper presented at the Sixth BDA International Conference on Dyslexia, York, UK.

Dunn, R. & Dunn, K. (1992) *Teaching Elementary Students through Their Individual Learning Styles*. Boston: Allyn & Bacon.

Dunn, R. & Dunn, K. (1993) *Teaching Secondary Students through Their Individual Learning Styles*. Boston: Allyn & Bacon.

Dunn, R., Dunn, K. & Price, G.E. (1989) *Learning Styles Inventory*. Lawrence, KS: Price Systems.

Dyslexia in Scotland (2002) The DDAT Centre: Another cure for dyslexia. Special edition of *Dyslexia in Scotland, Information Sheet*. Stirling, UK.

Everatt, J. (2002) Visual processes. In G. Reid & J. Wearmouth (Eds) *Dyslexia and Literacy: Theory and Practice*. Chichester: John Wiley & Sons.

Equazen Nutraceuticals (2004) *Fatty Acids and Learning Conditions. The Facts. The Benefits. The Evidence*. Equazen Nutraceuticals, 31 St Petersburg Place, London W2 4LA. www.equazen.com

Farquhar, S.-E. (2003) *Parents as Teachers First: A Study of the New Zealand PAFT Programme*. Wellington, NZ: Child Forum Research. www.childforum.com

Fawcett, A.J. & Nicolson, R.I. (1996) *The Dyslexia Screening Test*. London: The Psychological Corporation.

Fawcett, A.J. & Nicolson, R.I. (1997) *The Dyslexia Early Screening Test.* London: The Psychological Corporation.

Fawcett, A.J. & Nicolson, R.I. (2004) Dyslexia: The role of the cerebellum. In G. Reid & A. Fawcett (Eds) *Dyslexia in Context: Research, Policy and Practice.* London: Whurr.

Fawcett, A., Nicolson, R. & Lee, R. (2001) *The Pre-school Screening Test (PREST).* London: The Psychological Corporation.

Fife Education Authority (1996) *Partnership: Professionals, Parents and Pupils.* Scotland: Fife Education Authority.

Fisher, S.E., Marlow, A.J., Lamb, J., Maestrini, E., Williams, D.F., Richardson, A.J. et al. (1999) A quantitative-trait locus on chromosome 6p influences different aspects of developmental dyslexia. *American Journal of Human Genetics,* **64,** 146–156.

Fox, A. (1999) *Brain Gym.* Unpublished MEd dissertation. University of Edinburgh.

Galaburda, A. (1993a) *Cortical and sub-cortical mechanisms in dyslexia.* Paper presented at the Forty-fourth Annual Conference, Orton Dyslexia Society, New Orleans, LA.

Galaburda, A. (Ed.) (1993b) *Dyslexia and Development: Neurobiological Aspects of Extraordinary Brains.* Cambridge, MA: Harvard University Press.

Gilger, J.W., Pennnington, B.F. & DeFries, J.C. (1991) Risk for reading disability as a function of parental history in three family studies. *Reading and Writing,* **3** (3–4), 205–217.

Given, B. & Reid, G. (1999) *Learning Styles: A Guide for Teachers and Parents.* St Anne's, Lancashire: Red Rose Publications.

Goddard-Blythe, S. (1996) *Developmental Exercise Programme.* Chester, UK: Institute for Neuro-Physiological Psychology.

Goddard-Blythe, S. & Hyland, D. (1998) Screening for neurological dysfunction in the specific learning difficulties child. *British Journal of Occupational Therapy,* **61** (10), 459–464.

Government of Ireland (2001, July) *Republic of Ireland Report of the Task Force on Dyslexia.*

Harris, D.A. & MacRow-Hill, S.L. (1998) A comparative study with the intuitive colorimeter. *Optometry Today,* **38,** 15.

Healy, J.M. (1991) *Endangered Minds.* New York: Simon & Schuster.

Healy, J.M. (1994) *Your Child's Growing Mind.* New York: Doubleday Dell.

Helveston, E.M. (2001) Tinted lenses: A critique. *Perspectives,* **27** (3), 12–13.

HMG (1995) Disability Discrimination Act (1995). HMSO.

HMG (2001) Special Educational Needs and Disability Act (2001) (SENDA). HMSO.

Hornsby, B. (1996) *Before Alpha: Learning Games for the Under Fives.* London: Souvenir Press.

Irons, P. (2004) Scientific and non-technical papers from Tinta Vision. www.tintavisionj.com/sci papers.htm

Johanson, K. (1997) *Left hemisphere stimulation with music and sounds in dyslexia remediation.* Paper presented at the Forty-eighth Annual Conference of the International Dyslexia Association (formerly Orton Dyslexia Association), Baltimore, MD, USA.

Jordan, I. (2002) *Visual Dyslexia: Signs, Symptoms and Assessment.* North Lincolnshire: Desktop Publications. www.desktoppublications.co.uk

Lednicka, I. (2004) Families of children with dyslexia. Demanding life situations: stress and resiliency. PhD thesis, Charles University, Prague, August 2004.

Longdon, W. & Longdon, A. (2001) Brain Gym training. *News and Views.* Scottish Dyslexia Trust Newsletter (Spring).

Longdon, A. & Longdon, B. (2004, May) Brain Gym® in Schools: An update. *The Magazine of Dyslexia, Scotland.* Stirling, Scotland.

Mackay, N. (2004) The case for dyslexia-friendly schools. In G. Reid & A. Fawcett (Eds) *Dyslexia in Context: Research, Policy and Practice.* London: Whurr.

Marshall, A. (2003) *Brain Scans show Dyslexics Read Better with Alternative Strategies.* Kent: Davis® Dyslexia Association. davisUK@dyslexia.com

Mathews, M. (1993) *Can children be helped by applied kinesiology?* Paper presented at the Fifth European Conference in Neuro-Developmental Delay in Children with Specific Learning Difficulties, Chester, UK.

McIntyre, C. (2001) *Dyspraxia 5–11.* London: David Fulton Publications.

McLoughlin, D. (2004) Dyslexia and the workplace: Policy for an inclusive society. In G. Reid & A. Fawcett (Eds) *Dyslexia in Context* (pp. 177–188) London: Whurr.

McLoughlin, D., Fitzgibbon, G. & Young, V. (1994) *Adult Dyslexia: Assessment, Counselling and Training.* London: Whurr.

McLoughlin, D., Leather, C. & Stringer, P. (2002) *The Adult Dyslexic: Interventions and Outcomes.* London: Whurr.

McPhillips, M., Hepper, P.G. & Mulhern, G. (2000) Effects of replicating primary-reflex movements on specific reading difficulties in children: A randomised double-blind, controlled trial. *Lancet,* **355,** 537–541.

Miles, T.R. (2003) Commentary on the Reynolds et al. article. *Dyslexia,* **9** (2), 122–123.

Nicolson, R.I. & Fawcett, A.J. (1990) Automaticity: A new framework for dyslexia research? *Cognition,* **35,** 159–182.

Nicolson, R.I. & Reynolds, D. (2003, May) Sound findings and appropriate statistics: Response to Snowling and Hulme. *Dyslexia*, **9** (2), 134–135.

Nicolson, R.I., Fawcett, A.J. & Dean, P. (2001) Developmental dyslexia. The cerebellar deficit hypothesis. *Trends in Neurosciences*, **24** (9), 508–511.

Northern Ireland Education Dept (2002) *Task Group Report on Dyslexia*. Belfast.

Portwood, M. (2001) *Developmental Dyspraxia: A Practical Manual for Parents and Professionals*. Madeleine Durham County Council Educational Psychology Service, County Hall, Durham.

Pugh, N. (2003) Managing the system: How parents can make it happen. In M. Johnson & L. Peer (Eds) *The Dyslexia Handbook 2004*, pp. 277–281.

Reid, G. (2001) Specialist Teacher Training in the UK: Issues, considerations and future directions. In M. Hunter-Carsch (Ed.) *Dyslexia, A Psychosocial Perspective*. London: Whurr.

Reid, G. (2003) *Dyslexia: A Practitioner's Handbook*. Chichester: John Wiley & Sons.

Reid, G. & Kirk, J. (2001) *Dyslexia in Adults: Education and Employment*. Chichester: John Wiley & Sons.

Reid, G., Deponio, P. & Davidson-Petch, L. (2004) *Scotland-wide Audit of Education Authority Early Years Policies and Provision regarding Specific Learning Difficulties (SpLD) and Dyslexia*. Edinburgh: SEED.

Reid Lyon, G. (1998) Statement of Dr G. Reid Lyon, Chief Child Development and Behavior Branch, National Institute of Child Health and Human Development, National Institute of Health, to the Committee on Labor and Human Resources, Room 430, Senate Dirkson Building, Washington, DC, 28 April 1998. http://www.readbygrade3.com/readbygrade3co/lyon.htm

Reid Lyon, G., Shaywitz, S.E., Chhabra, V. & Sweet, R. (2004) Evidence-based reading policy in the US. In G. Reid & A. Fawcett (Eds) *Dyslexia in Context: Research, Policy and Practice*. London: Whurr.

Reynolds, D., Nicolson, R.I. & Hambly, H. (2003) Evaluation of an exercise-based treatment for children with reading difficulties. *Dyslexia*, **9** (1), 48–71.

Richardson, A.J. (2001) *Dyslexia, dyspraxia and ADHD – Can nutrition help?* Paper presented at the Fourth Cambridge Conference, Helen Arkell Dyslexia Association (March), Cambridge.

Richardson, A.J. & Puri, B.K. (2000) The potential role of fatty acids in attention deficit/hyperactivity disorder (ADHD). *Prostaglandins Leukotr. Essent. Fatty Acids*, **63**, 79–87.

Robertson, J. & Bakker, D.J. (2002) The Balance Model of Reading and Dyslexia. In G. Reid & J. Wearmouth (Eds) *Dyslexia and Literacy: Theory and Practice*. Chichester: John Wiley & Sons.

Scott, L., McWinnie, H., Taylor, L., Stevenson, N., Irons, P., Lewis, E. et al. (2002) Coloured overlays in schools: Orthoptic and optometric findings. *Ophthalmic and Physiological Optometry*, **22**, 156–165.

SEED (2004) Education (Additional Support for Learning) (Scotland) Bill. Edinburgh: HMSO.

Silver, L. (2001) Controversial therapies. In *Perspectives* (Summer), **27** (3), 1–4. Baltimore: IDA.

Singleton, C.H. (1996) *COPS 1 Cognitive Profiling System*. Nottingham: Chameleon Educational Ltd (now Beverley, East Yorkshire: Lucid Creative Ltd).

Singleton, C.H. (2002) Dyslexia: Cognitive factors and implications for literacy. In G. Reid & J. Wearmouth (Eds) *Dyslexia and Literacy: Theory and Practice*. Chichester: John Wiley & Sons.

Singleton, C.H. (2003) Cognitive factors and implications for literacy. In G. Reid & J. Wearmouth (Eds) *Dyslexia and Literacy: Theory and Practice*. Chichester: John Wiley & Sons.

Singleton, C.H., Horne, J.K. & Thomas, K.V. (1999) Computerised baseline assessment of literacy. *Journal of Research in Reading*, **22**, 67–80.

Singleton, C.H., Horne, J.K. & Thomas, K.V. (2002) *Lucid Adult Dyslexia Screening (LADS)*. Beverley, East Yorkshire: Lucid Creative Ltd.

Snowling, M.J. (2000) *Dyslexia* (2nd edn). Oxford: Blackwell.

Snowling, M.J. & Hulme, C. (2003) A critique of claims from Reynolds, Nicolson and Hambly (2003) that DDAT is an effective treatment for children with reading difficulties – 'Lies, Damned Lies and (Inappropriate) Statistics?' *Dyslexia*, **9** (2), 127–133.

Stein, J. (2003) Evaluation of an exercise-based treatment for children with reading difficulties. *Dyslexia*, **9** (2), 124–126.

Stein, J. (2004) Dyslexia genetics. In G. Reid & A. Fawcett (Eds) *Dyslexia in Context: Research, Policy and Practice*. London: Whurr.

Tannock, R. (1976) Doman–Delacato method for treating brain injured children. *Physiotherapy*, **28** (4).

Task Force on Dyslexia (2001) *Report*. Dublin: Government Publications. Available on-line at http://www.irlgov.ie/educ/pub.htm

Taylor, M.F. (1998) *An evaluation of the effects of educational kinesiology (Brain Gym®) on children manifesting ADHD in a South African context*. Unpublished MPhil dissertation. University of Exeter, UK.

Taylor, M.F. (2002) *Stress-induced atypical brain lateralization in boys with attention-deficit/hyperactivity disorder. Implications for scholastic performance*. Unpublished PhD thesis. University of Western Australia, Perth, Australia.

Terras, M., Minnis, H., Mackenzie, E. & Thomson, L. (2004) *'I feel very, very small': Reflections on living with dyslexia*. Poster presentation at the Sixth International BDA Conference, Warwick (March 2004).

UNESCO (1994) Salamanca Statement. Spain.

US Department of Education (2002) Office of Vocational and Adult Education, Division of Adult Education and Literacy (Learning Disabilities and Spanish-speaking Adult Populations): *The Beginning of a Process*. Washington, DC.

US Department of Education (2003, May) Office of Special Education and Rehabilitative Services (OSERS) Longitudinal Study of the Vocational Rehabilitation Services Program, Final Report 2: *VR Services and Outcomes, Rehabilitation Services Administration*, Chapter IV, pp. 4–7. Washington, DC. ED Contract No. HR92022001.

US Government (2001a) Full Funding of the Individuals with Disabilities Education Act (2001). Washington, DC.

US Government (2001b) Reauthorization of the Elementary and Secondary Education Act (2001). Washington, DC.

US Government (2001c) No Child Left Behind Act (2001). Washington, DC.

Weedon, C. & Reid, G. (2003) *Special Needs Assessment Profile*. London: Hodder & Stoughton. www.SNAPassessment.com

West, T.G. (1991/1997) *In the Mind's Eye. Visual Thinkers, Gifted People with Learning Difficulties, Computer Images and the Ironies of Creativity*. Buffalo, NY: Prometheus Books.

Wilkins, A. (2003) *Reading Through Colour. How Colour Filters can Reduce Reading Difficulty, Eye Strain and Headaches*. Chichester: John Wiley & Sons.

Wilkins, A.J., Jeanes, J.R., Pumfrey, P.D. & Laskier, M. (1996) *Rate of Reading Test R: Its Reliability, and its Validity in the Assessment of the Effects of Coloured Overlays*. MRC Applied Psychology Unit, 15 Chaucer Road, Cambridge.

Wilkins, A.J., Patel, R., Adjamian, R. & Evans, B.J.W. (2002) Tinted spectacles and visually sensitive migraine. *Cephalalgia*, **22** (9), 711–719.

Young, G. & Browning, J. (2004) Learning disability/dyslexia and employment. In G. Reid & A. Fawcett (Eds) *Dyslexia in Context: Research, Policy and Practice*. London: Whurr.

Index